THE CRITICAL INCIDENT IN GROWTH GROUPS: A MANUAL FOR GROUP LEADERS

THE CRITICAL INCIDENT IN GROWTH GROUPS: A MANUAL FOR GROUP LEADERS

by

ARTHUR M. COHEN, Ph.D.
Atlanta, Georgia

and

R. DOUGLAS SMITH, Ph.D.
Macon, Georgia

University Associates, Inc.
7596 Eads Avenue, La Jolla, California 92037

To Kenneth D. Benne and Warren G. Bennis,
teachers and friends

A special acknowledgment
to Carolyn M. Kilpatrick, M.Ed.,
colleague and friend,
without whose administrative
and technical contributions
this book would not have been published

Table of Contents

Structural Interventions

Introduction to This Manual

This manual is a companion volume to *The Critical Incident in Growth Groups: Theory and Technique*. The text deals with the history and evolution of groups, conditions for learning in groups, the Intervention Cube, the Critical-Incident Model and its use and applicability, and a theory of group growth and development. The Intervention Cube (Chapter 3) offers a unique model for analyzing interventions; when used in conjunction with the model for group growth and development (Chapter 5), it can help a group leader make more effective interventions, regardless of his theoretical orientation. The technique called the Critical-Incident Model (Chapter 4) is useful for organizing interactional data among group members.

Intended as an essential complement to the text, this manual offers the reader a specific, precise, detailed look at significant events—critical events—that typically occur in personal growth groups. This approach allows the user to read actual dialogues, to pinpoint the exact moment of the critical incident, to consider how he would respond, to hear the tone and style of the authors' suggested interventions, and then to compare their approaches with his own. The format is that of a workbook, planned so that the user may select one critical incident or several in sequence.

This manual can be used for both research and training purposes. Various intervention styles can be evaluated with the Intervention Cube; group leaders may want to use the manual as a "What would you do?" written description of their styles or as a basis for role playing the critical incidents for training purposes.

The critical incidents presented are taken from over three hundred actual episodes that occurred in more than thirty personal growth groups observed over a six-year period. They were selected to reflect the diversity of issues facing a beginning or advanced group leader and can be generalized to a wide range of similar situations. The critical incidents portray common phenomena in growth groups; some are chosen because they illustrate especially difficult situations for the group leader; others are included because they depict crucial milestones in the life of a group.

1

The groups from which these critical incidents were taken represented a broad spectrum of members drawn from colleges and universities, different levels of government, churches, social services, and industry. Both men and women, ranging in age from 18 to 60, were included. The nature of the personal growth settings varied widely: from college and graduate classes whose groups met once or twice a week for two to four hours for one or more semesters; to week-long, live-in programs both for special groups and for the community as a whole. Each group lasted for a minimum of thirty hours; group size averaged ten to fourteen members; most groups had one facilitator, and some had two. The names of participants have been changed, and other clues that could be used to identify particular individuals or groups have been eliminated.

FORMAT OF INCIDENTS

The sixty-one critical incidents are arranged in chronological order, with thirty-four incidents from the beginning phase of a group, fourteen from the middle phase, and thirteen from the ending phase. Together, they constitute a narrative of significant interactions over the time span of a group.

Each critical incident is organized and arranged according to the Critical-Incident Model (described in Chapter 4 of the text). The basic components of the Critical-Incident Model are outlined and explained here. The complete model form is presented fully in the Appendix at the end of this manual.

Title. Each incident is labeled to indicate whether it most frequently occurs in the beginning (B), middle (M), or end (E) phase of a group. The title indicates the general motif of the incident.

Theme topic. Linked to the phase of group development in which the critical incident occurs, the theme topic indicates the basic issue or issues involved in the critical incident. (See Chapter 5, A Model of Group Growth and Development, in the text.) Some incidents may refer to several phases or topics simultaneously. A master index of theme topics, critical incidents, and optional structural interventions is described at the end of this introduction and presented in the Appendix.

Context of incident. A brief indication of the context within which each critical incident occurred is specified. The phase and, often, the approximate session number is noted; the prevailing climate is described; the person or persons involved are introduced; and any relevant past or current behavior is noted.

Event preceding choice point. This section carefully details the behavior, comment, or conversation that immediately preceded the choice point confronting the leader. He must base his decision—whether to make an intervention and, if so, what kind of intervention—on this specific occurrence.

Choice point. Presented here is a brief theoretical discussion of both the surface and the underlying issues perceived in the critical incident. Guidelines regarding pacing, timing, the maturity of the group, and other significant factors are also offered in this section.

What would you do at this point? Give rationale. The reader is invited to write down, verbatim, the intervention he would give in this critical incident, given the preceding information. If the intervention he chooses is nonverbal or structural, he should describe it in detail. A brief rationale for his choice should accompany the actual intervention.

The reader should use the Intervention Cube (Chapter 3 of the text) to classify his interventions according to *level* (personal, interpersonal, group), *type* (conceptual, experiential, structural), and *intensity* (low, medium, or high). Over a number of incidents, this classification will yield a description of the reader's intervention style.

Suggested intervention. In this section, the authors indicate their choice of an appropriate intervention or interventions and offer a classification of each according to level, type, and intensity.

An offered intervention represents *one* intervention, not necessarily the "right answer" or the "final word." The interventions stem from the authors' particular orientation; leaders from other orientations may suggest quite different interventions for any given critical incident. Regardless of a leader's orientation, however, the Intervention Cube offers a means of classifying and evaluating interventions and can help a leader make his interventions in more precise directions. (See Chapter 4 in the text for examples of the utility of this approach in widely differing groups.) The interventions suggested in this manual are presented for examination by the reader, to be compared and contrasted with the interventions he specified.

Intervention outcome. The aftermath of the intervention is described, the hoped-for results indicated, and the group's actual response reported.

USING THIS MANUAL

Trainers and trainees will find many ways to use this book, either independently or with the accompanying text. The entire sequence can be worked during a course, workshop, or continuing program on personal growth. Or several incidents can be selected to preface a discussion based on group themes, differences in theoretical approaches, or comparisons of leader styles. Leaders are invited to structure and compare critical incidents from their own experiences, using the format described here.

The intent of the authors in preparing this manual is to provide material that can be used to stimulate the group leader's creativity and increase his effectiveness.

Structural Interventions

All suggested structural interventions are grouped together at the end of this manual and described in terms of *when* each is to be used, *how* it is to be conducted, and the *results* to be expected. For each structural intervention, the specific critical incidents to which the structural intervention may be related are indicated. This cross-indexing allows the reader to learn first the verbal intervention used in a critical incident and then the suggested structural intervention, or to reverse the process if he is primarily concerned with structural interventions and their relationship to a theory of group process. (See Chapter 5.)

THE MASTER INDEX

In the Appendix is a master index that performs the following functions:

1. It lists and briefly describes the ten theme topics (group phases) that serve as the authors' model of group growth and development. (See Chapter 5.)

2. It specifies the critical incidents that best illustrate a specific theme topic. There are not less than five critical incidents for each theme topic. If a given theme topic is particularly complex and involves several factors, there may be up to sixteen critical incidents reflecting that specific phase. For each theme topic, at least one structural intervention that may be made by the group leader is suggested.

3. It indicates structural interventions that may effectively be introduced at the option of the group leader in order to clarify and/or facilitate the understanding of a given group issue or process. In other words, certain critical incidents may be better resolved or illustrated when followed by a structural intervention designed to highlight the just-completed process. In other critical incidents, no further activity is judged necessary.

As can be noted from the master index, some critical incidents may reflect at least two distinct theme topics (phases), rather than just one, because it often happens that a given group interaction may be a blending of two or more themes. In these instances, the critical incident has been noted in the master index by an asterisk, indicating that it is to be found in another theme topic as well. Critical Incident B-2, for example, represents the theme topics of both "acquaintance" and "goal ambiguity and diffuse anxiety" and is listed under both theme topics. Thirteen of the sixty-one critical incidents illustrate more than one theme topic. (Each theme topic pertaining to a specific critical incident is listed at the beginning of that critical incident.)

SUMMARY STATEMENT

It should be noted again that the authors' suggested interventions are intended to be guidelines, rather than final words. The interventions chosen by a psychoanalytic, nondirective, encounter, or rational-therapist leader may all be different, depending upon the orientation of each. The authors do not advocate an uncritical imitation of their responses and their "leadership style," but rather suggest the adoption of a philosophical attitude and a prescribed thrust and approach to the ambiguous area of interventions.

The authors believe that the approach they suggest will offer a means of conceptualizing and objectifying the frequently confusing bombardment of stimuli that impinge on the leader in a group. Equally, they believe that this approach will offer a personal source of stability for the group leader who is struggling with his own sense of anxiety in the group. The authors disagree with those who feel that the beginning group leader's anxiety, struggle, and floundering are necessary and indispensable to his personal growth—almost an end in themselves. How much anxiety and struggle is necessary and how much is nonproductive for both the leader and the group is an empirical question. The authors do not feel their approach will remove the anxiety and uncertainties inherent in group leadership; it will, however, give the group leader more effective tools to shape his own personal style and impact on the group.

BEGINNING CRITICAL INCIDENTS

Critical Incident B-1: Going Around

Theme Topic: Acquaintance

Context of Incident

This is the first group session. The general climate of the group is a mixture of awkwardness and anxiety, members being unsure of their direction and unfamiliar with one another. A few dependency statements have been made to the group by particularly anxious members, but there has been little response. One group member, who appears somewhat more aggressive, has apparently decided to initiate some action as he begins speaking in a loud, authoritative voice.

Event Preceding Choice Point

Alan: "Well, I think we should know something about ourselves. Let's go around the room and tell something about ourselves. You know, introduce ourselves and tell where we are from."

Bert: "That's a great idea. Why don't you start?"

The group picks up on this idea and continues until everyone is finished. It is now your turn, and everyone is watching you expectantly. What are the issues involved and the response alternatives available to you as a leader?

Choice Point

The surface issue in this critical incident is a simple suggestion involving members getting to know each other via names and professions. As such,

7

it serves the useful purpose of attaching a name to a face and identifying similar interests, and it is a general "ice-breaker." At another level, however, some members could care less about the background data of other members and are mostly concerned with trying to "fill up the time and break the silence." If the latter situation is occurring, it is helpful for the group leader to reflect on the underlying reasons for the group's behavior, in terms of feelings and issues. Since this is likely to be the group's first introduction to the dynamics behind a seemingly logical and straightforward process, the leader should introduce his observations as nonjudgmentally and descriptively as possible in order to provide the group members with an opportunity both to participate and to observe the issues in that experience. This should be the start of an elaborate training process that must provide the knowledge, skills, and values the group will need to be able, in time, to assume distributive leadership functions.

What would you do at this point? Give rationale.

Suggested Interventions

The intervention for this beginning-phase critical incident is almost always at the group level unless the group leader is directly confronted by a particular individual.

The group leader may remain quiet, looking comfortably at the group members, frustrating their expectations for guidance and allowing the anxiety to build within the group. (Group level, experiential type, low to medium intensity.)

Or he may say, "I'd like to share some of my thoughts with you about how I feel right now. I'm feeling pretty boxed in and a little uncertain as to how I should reply." (Group level, experiential type, low intensity, involving sharing feelings and modeling behavior.) "On one hand, I hear you asking for some straight information and I'm certainly willing to give that, but I also hear each of us trying to feel each other out, to locate our personal boundaries and limitations, to categorize and pigeonhole, to fill up the silence and give ourselves some sort of temporary direction." (Group level, predominantly conceptual type, low intensity, giving a general but relatively superficial interpretation of both the surface and underlying issues. This introduces the concept of the "double message.") "I wonder if the rest of you feel that you really know each other that much better now? What sort of characteristics did we reveal about ourselves? Was this what we needed to know about that person?" (Group level, conceptual type, low intensity.) This intervention encourages the sharing of ideas and feelings about the just-finished process.

The group leader, as a resource person, has the option of introducing a structural intervention to encourage openness and cohesion among group members. The leader's decision to utilize such an exercise will be determined by his knowledge of individual group members and their needs, the speed with which he would like to see the group consolidate its gains, and the importance he attaches to structural interventions. Several typical and appropriate structured experiences are listed at the end of this critical incident to illustrate the potentially increased effectiveness of combining a variety of leadership approaches.

Intervention Outcome

Silence on the part of the leader usually serves the purpose of increasing the anxiety in the group to the point where it can no longer be ignored. This, in turn, may lead one or more members to comment on—and possibly explore—the sources of their anxiety. However, silence may result in a group member's finally asking, "Tell us a little about yourself, so we can get to know you." The group leader may then choose to respond with the preceding intervention. It can be seen from this example that the selection of a certain alternative (remaining silent) leads to a sequence of chained critical incidents, in which the probable future behavior of the group may be predicted by the nature of the intervention previously made.

The first verbal intervention by the leader is almost always of a low intensity during this stage of the group to minimize the threatening aspects of full group participation. Several major concepts and issues are introduced as having specific relevance for the group, e.g., the double message and the issues of anxiety, group intimacy, and inclusion. The introduction of these issues may spur discussion and recognition when they emerge in the future. Since the group members may have a heightened sense of dependency, due to the unstructured group situation, "modeling" the appropriate behavior by the leader becomes quite important as a source of imitation. In this manner, the acquisition of skills by the members is encouraged.

If a structural intervention is used, it could increase the level of intimacy among members in the group. Since members often share a large amount of personal background data, group cohesion is accelerated, and close member friendships are often initiated.

Optional Structural Interventions

1. Empathic Communication, p. 205
2. Early Perceptions, p. 207
3. The Sharing Progression, p. 209

Critical Incident B-2: Light Conversation

Theme Topics: Acquaintance
Goal Ambiguity and Diffuse Anxiety

Context of Incident

This critical incident, which occurs during the early phases of group life, focuses on the initial lack of direction group members face. Even with some direction and purpose, members often seek to avoid or delay coming to grips with their anxiety by dealing with topics that are trivial and have little personal relevance. The prevailing climate is a mixture of uncertainty, anxiety, and even boredom. In addition, among even the most verbal participants, there may be lengthening periods of silence that often develop into a particular style.

Event Preceding Choice Point

Carole: "Oh, you're a stock broker. Can you tell me how stocks work?"

or

Dave: "Did you read in the paper last night that J. A. Prufrock is running for mayor? What do all of you think about that?"

or

Edie: "Did anyone see that special on TV last night? It was great! What did you think . . . ?"

Choice Point

This interchange involves a number of issues. First, anxiety-eliciting topics are avoided by prolonged silences and interesting but irrelevant questions. While the surface issue appears to be one of seeking information and getting acquainted, the underlying issues center about strategies designed to avoid disclosure, to seek some sort of direction, or to evade personal confrontation. In general, this escape behavior or digression is of two types, each type requiring a different intervention.

11

What would you do at this point? Give rationale.

Suggested Interventions

The first intervention calls attention to the irrelevance of what the group members are saying and directs them to consider why they are trying to escape involvement via this route.

Group Leader: "You know, for the last twenty minutes or so, we've talked about baseball, puberty rights, gardening, and the role of the counter-culture in society. And when we start this shifting, like a bee going from flower to flower, and do it so intently, it indicates that something's going on here that we'd just as soon not deal with. The biggest thing that I can see that exists in a group like ours, at this point, is our own feelings about each other and just being in the group." (Group level, conceptual type, low intensity.) The intervention begins with a simple description of ongoing events. It then interprets those events by acknowledging an underlying issue of anxiety over disclosure and intimacy.

However, the group discussion may not really be irrelevant conversation. The group, for example, may be talking about the difficulties that younger people have in dealing with unstructured situations—a subject that might occur when people, on a surface level, are apparently talking in a digressive manner about how they are feeling at an underlying process level. In this case, the intervention is quite different from the first.

Group Leader: "You know, it's been my observation that, a lot of times, groups talk on a content level about things that reflect how they're feeling underneath. And they do this without saying much directly. For example, for about twenty minutes we've been talking about how young people might find it difficult to deal with unstructured situations. I can't help but feel that we're really talking about ourselves, and that we are facing the very dilemma we've been talking about. Except that it's here and now. What, exactly, is it that we do with what's going on—this lack of structure? Obviously one way we've taken in the last twenty minutes is to deal with the lack of structure by talking about the lack of structure—thereby not having to deal directly with our feelings about it. How do the rest of you feel?" (Group level, conceptual type, low intensity.) This statement focuses directly on the underlying process events and how they are reflected in the ongoing conversation.

Intervention Outcome

Unless the group is especially receptive, there may be either polite acceptance of the intervention statement or massive denial of any underlying concerns. Usually a group will exhibit both of these situations, to a mixed degree. The suggested intervention may also open doors for many group members to respond to authority in much the same manner as they have in the past, i.e., with hostility, dependency, indifference, and so forth. If the response from a group member is an especially intense affirmation or denial, the group leader may then stimulate further exploration by an additional intervention:

"When I get the kind of response that just happened, I have the feeling that the observations were touching some pretty sensitive areas." (Group level, experiential type, low intensity.) This usually precipitates further awareness of the relationship of process to actual observed behavior.

Critical Incident B-3: Ignored Request

Theme Topics: Acquaintance
Sharpened Affects and Anxieties:
Increased Defensiveness

Context of Incident

This event occurs during the beginning of the group's life. The group members are in an exploratory, anxious, wandering phase and have not yet learned to deal with the needs of individual group members. One group member, who is quite anxious, makes a request of the group. The request is ignored and the group abruptly starts out in a new direction, discussing other topics.

Event Preceding Choice Point

Frank: "Let's discuss things in the group that keep us from knowing each other. I'd like to see us start by telling what we dislike most."

There is a moment of silence; then the group starts off on another topic as if Frank's statement had not been made.

Choice Point

The surface issue appears to be a legitimate request on the part of one member, which was subsequently ignored by the group. Care must be taken, however, to understand the nature of the request—in this instance a request for personal information. The above situation is best known as a "plop-flop," i.e., a member's comment, request, or attempt at influence that receives little or no response from other members. To all apparent purposes, the comment has been thrown into unresponsive waters—hence a plop-flop. The major underlying issues are those of disclosure, intimacy, and denial by avoidance on the part of the group. Other important surface issues are group responsibility toward the individual and the legitimacy of certain topics for discussion. Perhaps Frank's suggestion was too threatening and aroused too

14

much anxiety in other members. Perhaps Frank was attempting to establish norms of openness and intimacy that other, more conservative, members were resisting. (Sharpened anxieties: increased defensiveness.) Regardless of the exact nature of the issues involved, the phenomenon should be recognized, discussed, and understood in the light of the ongoing group processes. The judgment of the leader is essential in choosing the issue or issues that appear largely to account for this phenomenon at any given time.

What would you do at this point? Give rationale.

Suggested Intervention

It is suggested that the leader remain silent initially to allow group members to comment on this problem, i.e., to let the group experience the sense of impotence and frustration of one of their members. Following this, if no one comments on what has happened, the leader may intervene at the group level and briefly conceptualize the plop-flop phenomenon as well as invite members to respond to it. This intervention would serve the purpose of encouraging norms concerned with a sense of shared frustration and group responsibility.

Another intervention would be to respond directly to the comment made by the group member.

Group Leader: "Frank, let me tell you how I feel about that. I think we are working on some pretty important issues about relationships, and I, too, would like to pick up on your topic, but it's my feeling that some other members aren't ready for this. I'm disagreeing with you, but I want you to know I heard your request and I'm not ignoring you." (Individual level, experiential type, low intensity.)

The intervention models the legitimacy of disagreeing with another member, while at the same time recognizing and maintaining respect for his position.

A final suggested intervention would be addressed to the entire group.

Group Leader: "You know, Frank expressed an opinion about the direction that he would like to see the group follow and no one responded. Instead we picked up on something else, a plop-flop." (Group level, conceptual type, low intensity.) "I don't know about you, but I'm feeling kind of strained and awkward, because it's happened to me in the past, and I'm sure it will happen to others in the future." (Group level, experiential type, medium intensity.) "People seem to have several different ways of handling this situation: they can pay no attention, as we just did. Or perhaps they might respond to Frank, even if they disagree, by just picking up on his comments." (Group level, conceptual type, low intensity.) "Let me ask you, Frank. How did you feel when the group didn't pick up or respond to your statement?" (Individual level, experiential type, low intensity.)

This intervention is designed to encourage Frank's expression of personal feelings as well as the comments of other group members.

Intervention Outcome

This chain of suggested interventions encourages the observation and resolution of the plop-flop phenomenon and the resulting feelings of anxiety and frustration. The resolution of this group process may take several forms, as outlined in the suggested interventions. The most important consequence of not picking up on a plop-flop is the member's sense of being alone and of lacking membership and control, as well as a feeling of being unimportant to the group. If time limitations permit, members should be urged to think of other group situations in which they have been caught in a plop-flop. This sharing of feelings about a frustrating experience should lead to greater emotional cohesion among members in the group and permit them to generalize their experience to other group situations.

Optional Structural Interventions

1. Empathic Communication, p. 205
2. Early Perceptions, p. 207

Critical Incident B-4: Head Trip

Theme Topic: Acquaintance

Context of Incident

This is one of the early group sessions. Many of the members, in an attempt to allay anxiety over lack of structure, have started discussions on topics dealing with life, death, current world concerns, and so forth. The general climate is one of an academic gathering, with observers and participants ostensibly engaged in intellectual discourse. As soon as one topic has been discussed, another is taken up. This behavior is satisfying acquaintance needs, as well as providing temporary direction for the group members. One female group member who has dominated the discussion in an emotional manner often glances covertly to the group leader as if to gauge his responses. She is finishing a rather long monologue in which she has stated that any relationship, especially marriage, needs to be solidified by a contract, to avoid chaos. Other members have been variously agreeing or disagreeing.

Event Preceding Choice Point

Gloria: "And that's why I think a formal contract with rules should be established. Otherwise, a couple would not be bound together—no one would. Lack of any kind of guidelines makes it very hard on a couple . . . " She pauses and looks at the other group members.

Choice Point

The surface issue appears to be the straightforward emotional expression of a topic of current interest. Ostensibly, it is a means for members to get to know one another through the medium of expressed attitudes and opinions. However, Gloria's posture, along with the emotional tone of her verbalizations, suggests that the topic may be serving more than just the process of acquaintance. On an underlying level, the topics of contracts and enduring

18

relationships may be directly related to the issues of goal ambiguity and diffuse anxiety. Since the leader does not know whether this is a valid assumption, his intervention should be couched in nonthreatening terms as a hypothesis rather than as a stated fact.

What would you do at this point? Give rationale.

Suggested Intervention

The first suggested intervention involves a frank comment on the surface issue.

Group Leader: "It seems that there are some pretty strong feelings aroused by the topics we have chosen. Discussing emotionally charged topics may be one of the ways we get closer and get to know one another better. Often, at this stage in the life of a group, we are not ready to express our feelings directly to one another, and so we may choose a topic that is outside of the immediate group through which we can vent our feelings. Does anyone else feel this way, or have a comment?" (Group level, conceptual type, low intensity.)

Another approach would be to comment directly on the underlying issues. Direct comment will increase the group's anxiety and defensiveness if presented in a threatening manner. However, a nonthreatening direct comment may serve to sensitize the group to future underlying issues and to the fact that surface discussions are often distortions of underlying, very real concerns.

Group Leader: "Gloria, in addition to expressing your views on the topic of formal vs. informal marriage, I wonder if many of us aren't really talking about things that concern us in here—such as whether we should have formal rules spelled out, in order to grow and become productive, or whether we should try to accept the lack of rules as a sign of failure for the group. Is it really just an academic discussion—or are we in large part talking about our concerns for structure, here and now in the group?" (Individual level, conceptual type, medium intensity, shifting to group level. The purpose of this shift is to encourage response from many members.)

Intervention Outcome

The two interventions described above may have a common effect: tactfully to introduce the concept that things are not always what they seem and that it is possible to discuss one topic as a defensive maneuver to avoid talking about another, more threatening, topic. The major contrast between the two interventions is one of directness and specificity. The first intervention simply suggests that the group behavior represents attempts to handle anxiety and the acquaintance process through the indirect discussion of topics, while the second specifies the type of anxiety and probes some possible underlying origins. The primary object of both interventions is to stimulate the exploration of various levels of group activity.

Optional Structural Intervention

4. Introspection, p. 211

Critical Incident B-5: Pessimistic Gloom

Theme Topic: Acquaintance

Context of Incident

This is an early to middle group session. Gradually the topic of trust, intimacy, and risk taking has emerged. As the group begins to realize that the ever-deepening acquaintanceship process may involve personal disclosure and sharing at an interpersonal level, some members may become frightened and defensive. They may seek to deny or block this movement by obvious ploys such as changing topics, missing meetings, taking serious discussions in a frivolous manner, conceptualizing and abstracting excessively, etc. At other times, group members may directly face their ambivalence and express it as a pessimistic outlook.

Following several such pessimistic statements by various group members, along with verbalizations dealing with the difficulty of trusting others, a generally gloomy prediction of the group's future is offered by Hank. He vacillates between being dependent and counterdependent and often attempts to be a co-leader.

Event Preceding Choice Point

Hank: "So what I guess I'm saying is that I think we have an impossible task. I don't think I'm going to trust anyone in this group completely in nine weeks. It just . . . I don't know . . . can't probably be done."

Following this statement, other group members nod their heads pessimistically. There follows a long period of silence.

Choice Point

The surface issue concerns itself with the realistic possibilities of attaining a deeper level of acquaintance in a fixed amount of time. At first glance, it may seem to be a realistic attempt to assess the extent of involvement. On a deeper level, it may be a reflection of the anxiety and ambivalence of members when faced with the potential threat of closer, more intimate relationships. The group leader must decide whether the reflection of the surface or underlying issue would best serve the group's needs.

What would you do at this point? Give rationale.

Suggested Intervention

Generally speaking, avoiding intense overinterpretations in the beginning stages of group life is recommended, since overinterpretation may "freeze" or inhibit the natural spontaneity that is beginning to emerge. In the initial stages, interventions should establish a supportive and freed-up atmosphere.

Group Leader: "What I hear you, Hank, and some of the rest of you, saying is reminiscent of a fantasy I just had: it's as if you were a gang of laborers with a huge pile of dirt to shovel, but you're all standing around, leaning on your shovels, talking. One of you says: 'Gee, do you think we'll ever get that moved?' Another says 'Gosh, I don't know.' In the meantime, it seems like we've been leaning on our shovels trying to decide!" (Group level, conceptual type, low intensity.)

Intervention Outcome

The above intervention is delivered in a humorous manner, with the humor covering a potent approach to describing the group style as it is currently operating. No attempt is made to interpret underlying issues or the anxiety that may be generated. Instead, a light-hearted metaphor is used gently to nudge the group into looking at itself. Nervous laughter may follow this intervention, as well as productive discussion on the current group style. Humor, in this instance, illustrates the relief of anxiety as well as support and reassurance.

Optional Structural Interventions

3. The Sharing Progression, p. 209
5. Surrender and Support, p. 213
6. The Group Slap, p. 215

Critical Incident B-6: What Is Proper?

Theme Topic: Goal Ambiguity and Diffuse Anxiety

Context of Incident

During the early stages of group life, there is a climate of uncertainty and anxiety developing around the lack of formality and structured goals. This uncertainty and ambiguity may motivate certain group members to ask probing questions that reflect their concerns. These questions usually deal with such issues as dependency and attempt to reduce tension by acquiring knowledge. There are also implicit questions that underlie the surface question: concerns over "proper" or "correct" group norms of behavior.

Event Preceding Choice Point

Inez (to group leader): "I've always heard from others and read in books that sensitivity groups required everyone to discuss very personal issues. Is that true?"

The group now waits for the leader's response.

Choice Point

Inez's statement may reflect fear of such groups and a wish to be reassured as to the nature of the present group, or perhaps she is actively seeking a group that discusses personal issues. Her further statements, as well as her tone of voice, usually reveal her basic attitude toward such groups. In many instances, a question of this nature is less a surface request for information than an underlying question designed to reduce diffuse anxiety and uncertainty. The issues of concern deal with goal ambiguity, intimacy, and self-disclosure as well as resistance to self-exploration.

What would you do at this point? Give rationale.

Suggested Intervention

Group Leader: "You know, I think the question you're raising is an important one. I wonder, however, why you're directing it at me, instead of at the other group members. Maybe what's just happened between us is a reflection of something more general going on. Usually society provides us with rules that are imposed from the outside. And what you're doing here is asking me to provide that same kind of service, which I'm not doing. And the question is, is it possible to generate a set of activities, a group process that will reflect what we all individually want? Can we make a world, or at least a small community that way? One that really works? Doing this involves some risk, some personal risk taking, since there will be no outside arbitrary force to guide each step you take. Only the force of members in a group, taking risks, forging their own direction. This is where we are now. Will we discuss personal things? I don't know. I wonder if it will be possible to build our group on the basis of a healthy balance between individual rights and group direction." (Individual level, conceptual type, medium intensity.)

This intervention was directed at one individual throughout the response sequence, but it is sufficiently general to allow applicability to the entire group. In this intervention, in addition, there was a brief input on the need for the group to discover its own emerging norms and standards as a measure of growth, rather than to allow an outside authority to lay down rules of disclosure or nondisclosure. In this manner, general guidelines are established for the group while, at the same time, the rights and anxieties of individual members are recognized and respected.

Intervention Outcome

The thrust of this intervention is to provide a broad framework within which members can begin to struggle together to establish some standards for group membership and participation. Answering a simple "yes" or "no" to a group member's question such as the previous one ignores the real value to be gained by each member as he struggles to build a community based on a consensus of need. Out of the ability of each member to assume responsibility for direction, standards, and values arises the real value of the experience: the opportunity both to participate in the ongoing process and, at the same time, to observe and study it. This intervention may encourage a subsequent discussion of group members' individual anxieties, of the need to decide upon ground rules and norms, and finally of the projected goals of the group.

Critical Incident B-7: Show Us the Way

Theme Topic: Goal Ambiguity and Diffuse Anxiety

Context of Incident

This critical incident usually emerges during the beginning of group life when there is anxiety and confusion over the correct group direction. The group members at this point usually express statements reflecting both a need for dependency and direction and feelings of resentment toward the group leader for not telling them what to do. The statements are a way of asking for goals, proper procedure, and directed leadership. The incident may arise at the very beginning of a session, or it may occur after a number of nonproductive "starts" on the part of the group.

Event Preceding Choice Point

Jack (to group leader): "We're not getting anything done! Could you tell us something to do to get us started? A topic or issue, maybe?"

Choice Point

The surface issue involves a legitimate request for information and guidance. The underlying issue involves the responsibilities of group members in determining their own direction, in spite of the increasing amount of diffuse anxiety this generates. The group leader should determine if his resources might best be used by urging the group to continue casting about for direction, or whether he should promote inquiry into appropriate areas by direct suggestion.

What would you do at this point? Give rationale.

Suggested Intervention

Group Leader (choosing to promote inquiry): "I think you're right, Jack. We've had some frustration and difficulties in deciding what we ought to be doing—and this seems to be pretty usual at this point. Ordinarily, people have some socially sanctioned procedure to fall back on—like Robert's Rules of Order. But we don't have one yet, and one of the problems we are going to have to face is how we make decisions—particularly as they affect our life together. This will involve being able to observe and participate at the same time—a sort of participant observer. Perhaps in this way we can arrive at some procedures for working together." (Begins at individual level, experiential type, low intensity and then concludes at group level, conceptual type, low intensity.)

The group leader may wish to utilize a structural intervention to facilitate a participant-observer orientation.

The object of this intervention is to structure the group loosely, thus offering group members an opportunity to solve their dilemma, without actually giving them answers or telling them exactly what to do. The goal ambiguity and diffuse anxiety is intended to motivate the group members to look at their own behavior and processes and determine their own goals as they develop. To offer a quick and easy solution to their anxiety would increase dependency and decrease any motivation for self-determination.

Intervention Outcome

The suggested verbal intervention recognized the frustrations stemming from the inability to understand or deal with group process. The structural intervention provided the group with a skill, a method of analysis, by utilizing a participant-observer approach. The group leader may be seen as having given in to the dependency demands of the group members. However, a distinction must be drawn between group members who already possess knowledge and skills they are unwilling to use and those members who need to be supplied with certain skills before they can function effectively. This critical incident is an example of the latter instance and is an approach that group members may utilize again at a later time in the group.

Optional Structural Intervention

7. Group Observing Group, p. 217

Critical Incident B-8: Seeking Approval

Theme Topics: Goal Ambiguity and Diffuse Anxiety
Members' Search for Position/Definition:
Primary Group Transferences/
Countertransferences

Context of Incident

This critical incident occurs during the very earliest stages of group life, especially when group members are concerned with issues of direction and guidance. Typically the climate is one of ambiguity and confusion, with one or more group members attempting to try out various suggestions made by other group members. This event usually occurs during the first or second session, and the exact nature of the group activity is not as important as the process of the group and individuals within the group, seeking a position of approval from the group leader.

Event Preceding Choice Point

Karen (following the group's involvement in some activity): "Is it permissible for group members to do this?"

The group members now turn and wait expectantly for the group leader's answer.

Choice Point

This event, which deals with the problem of dependency as well as with implied membership and norm issues, is a way of seeking approval and thereby determining if the group is progressing in the "correct" or "proper" direction. Consequently, it usually reveals more than just a simple surface request for information.

The underlying issues exhibit the prototype for a future series of encounters with authority. Either an affirmative or a negative answer to the question places the leader in the position of a "sanctioner" of the "correct pathways." The issue is not only an attempt to resolve goal ambiguity and diffuse anxiety; it may also demonstrate the process of members' searching for position in the group, perhaps by a pattern of dependency or counter-dependency statements directed toward the leader. The leader should therefore respond in a manner that will clarify the appropriate process and stimulate discussion.

What would you do at this point? Give rationale.

Suggested Intervention

Group Leader: "Karen, let me answer your question this way: I think we're beginning to struggle, at this phase of our life, with where controls over our behavior come from. Ordinarily, in our everyday life, we typically respond to external controls, and I could certainly be a logical agent of external control, though I don't really want to be. I guess the struggle we're having revolves around whether or not you have your own internal controls that would lead you to make your own decisions—and, most importantly, can others join you in exploring how we influence each other in a decision-making process? This is something we should all look at." (Group level, conceptual type, medium intensity.)

This conceptualization is basically a spontaneous theory input (see Chapter 3 of the text) involving issues of control, authority, influence, and decision making. As such, it provides a focal point for future discussion. A variation of this intervention would be to end the response differently:

Group Leader: "Karen, how do you feel about these things? I'd like to know what your sense of things might be." (Individual level, experiential type, low intensity.)

Intervention Outcome

This intervention began by pointing out the basic issues and concepts involved in answering an apparent request for information. The group, at this stage in its development, will not fully realize the implications of not being told the correct thing to do, of not being granted "permission." This intervention often paves the way for excellent discussions of the following topics: "How do we make decisions? What is our conditioned attitude toward authority?What do we do when thrown back upon our own resources?" By ending on an intervention at the individual level, however, the leader invites a repetition of the original request or more confusion and hostility on the part of the member making the request. In the former instance, the group leader would do well simply to repeat his intervention. In the latter instance, hostility is fully considered in other critical incidents to follow.

Critical Incident B-9: False Start

Theme Topic: Goal Ambiguity and Diffuse Anxiety

Context of Incident

This critical incident can occur during both the early and the middle stages of group life, when the group is generally too overcontrolled for productive work. Often, there is a noticeable increase in tension and anxiety among the group members, along with several "false starts." At other times, brief intellectual statements will be followed by long periods of silence. The few feelings that are brought out in the group are either ignored or intellectualized. This most often occurs during the beginning of a session. The climate appears to be one of both tension and withdrawal.

Event Preceding Choice Point

The group members, after several false starts, have lapsed into an uneasy silence. Members tend to avoid each other's eyes, and anxiety-based smiles break out from time to time.

Choice Point

Although silence can be a natural phenomenon, occurring when resources have been exhausted, this critical incident is primarily concerned with the appropriate handling of silence as an anxiety-motivated phenomenon. Silence may emerge as a reaction to conflict and tension that have been generated in the group; it involves a fear of losing control or overexposing one's emotions. The group leader has the option of letting the silence continue, thereby allowing enough anxiety to be generated so that the silence is broken by one or more members. If the group leader steps in too quickly or too often to break the silence with an intervention, the group may become dependent on the leader always to reduce its anxiety. The group must at times be encouraged to face and resolve its own anxieties. Silence, and the particular points at which it arises, may tell the group leader a great deal about the concerns and fears the members are experiencing. It may also define the points of resistance to further movement in the group, since silence may be defined as hostile, apathetic, etc. In this instance, the diffuse anxiety over the lack of clearly defined goals has increased to the point that no one is able to move effectively.

What would you do at this point? Give rationale.

Suggested Intervention

Group Leader (after deliberation): "I wonder if the silence and anxiety I sense has something to do with our attempts to deal with our feelings?" (Group level, experiential type, low intensity.)

There are two questions to be answered at this point: (1) what is an appropriate continuation of the above intervention? and (2) how is more silence to be handled? The continuation goes as follows:

Marleen: "I think you're right. I think there's something underneath going on that I don't know what to do about."

Noel: "Yeah, I don't want to say anything unless I'm sure it's relevant and that it's going to help the group. So, otherwise, I just try to keep my mouth shut."

Oscar: "Me, too. You know there are some people who are afraid that they'll feel stupid if they say something that really isn't brilliant. There are a lot of people like that."

Pam: "I think if we talked about ideas, you know, bring our ideas out and so forth . . . It's not as scary as talking about feelings. Just talk about our theoretical impressions of the group. I think that's how we ought to get the feelings, through ideas."

Quint: "Goals, if we had group goals, I think . . . "

Rose: "Yeah, and maybe . . . "

Group Leader: "A lot of issues and feelings have been hitting me during the last few minutes and I'd like to try to present a few impressions. I have a feeling that my statement of a few moments ago has implicitly encouraged some of you to act in order to get me to respond, or to 'cover the water-front.'" The important thing, I believe, is that a number of times people have mentioned some of their feelings and needs, and these needs have been almost deliberately ignored or ruled out. I think one of the things that all of you are doing is trying to get me to come in to relieve the pressures of having to come to grips with the sources of anxiety that you're having. It's like a 'game' and it goes something like this: when we feel tension and anxiety, we don't deal with it directly; we develop all kinds of mechanisms to avoid dealing with it. In another sense, we're talking about self-control; if we don't keep it in, we feel there would be hell to pay. Somebody might get hurt, maybe put down badly. So we beat about the bush and talk about what might happen. And we're really talking about ourselves! That's what we're struggling with, now. Each of us probably has a problem area, a concern that forces us to remain silent. The sources of our anxiety: How do we get them out, identify them, and use the help of others to get them worked through?" (Group level, conceptual type, high intensity.)

At this point, the leader has the option of inviting responses from all members about their fears and anxieties. Alternatively, he may suggest that everyone select someone in the group with whom he has not shared any real feelings and share them. These are only two possibilities.

Intervention Outcome

This intervention may encourage group members to look at sources of anxiety as an opportunity for personal growth. While there are a number of major and minor issues that could be recognized, the sharing of emotional concerns leads to greater group cohesion. Here, the silence was a reflection of underlying concerns only implicitly recognized by group members. If the leader's intervention generates anxiety leading to more silence, the above intervention pattern should be pressed more firmly. A structural intervention may be used at this point by asking everyone to write down his fears about the group, crumple the paper, and throw it into a pile in the middle of the circle. The leader then chooses a few papers at random and reads each response aloud, and everyone discusses the source of anxiety. This process is a type of verbal desensitization.

Critical Incident B-10: Loud Silence

Theme Topic: Members' Search for Position/Definition: Primary Group Transferences/ Countertransferences

Context of Incident

In the early stages of group life, when the climate is one of uncertainty and anxiety, long periods of silence are frequently observed. These periods of silence, which may come at the beginning of a group or at any time throughout the session, are a means of avoiding anxiety, but they finally begin to generate anxiety. This is sometimes termed a "flight into silence." This silence may be complete, in which no one speaks, or there may be sporadic attempts by group members to break the silence with one or two statements. These statements are usually followed by more silence while the group sits nervously looking at each other or at the group leader. Occasionally, anxiety-based laughter may erupt.

Event Preceding Choice Point

Sarah: "Well, are we going to just sit here without saying anything?" This may be followed by irrelevant conversation, or another group member may respond.

Tom (to group leader): "Why don't you tell us something to get us started?"

Choice Point

The first issue of this critical incident deals with the problem of silence and its meaning for the group. The second issue involves a confrontation with the leader and is basically a control and authority problem reflecting transference issues. Even if the question had been framed in a spirit of seeking information, it would indicate a lack of knowledge of the roles and responsibilities of both the group leader and the group members. Both these issues should be recognized and handled in the group leader's intervention response.

What would you do at this point? Give rationale.

Suggested Intervention

The first choice point occurs following Sarah's statement. The group leader obviously has the choice of responding or sitting quietly, frustrating the group's expectations. Here is where the trainer's own sense of judgment must be utilized. Our preference, in these situations, is for the group leader to remain silent. The leader would be doing a disservice to the group by prematurely reducing the level of anxiety. Anxiety, in these instances, may be used as a motivating force to spur future group interaction.

Tom's statement is more difficult to handle, although the group leader has the same option of remaining silent. The lack of a response on the leader's part would probably increase the group's discomfort and level of anxiety, leading to more frustration-generating responses. This is, however, certainly a reasonable approach to take. On the other hand, a suggested verbal intervention might be:

Group Leader: "It's pretty uncomfortable to sit here and not know what to do. By turning to me, a way is found to avoid or at least reduce the feelings of anxiety that have been building up. What are these anxieties? One might be the fear that you'll get hurt if you speak up or the fear of what other people might be thinking. Another is the fear of risk in saying things that others might laugh at. Would anyone care to share some of the hesitations you felt about what *might* have happened if you had spoken up during all that silence?" (Group level, conceptual/experiential type, medium intensity.)

The purpose of this intervention is to direct attention to the just-finished process in hopes that future occurrences will be recognized and handled appropriately by the group. The intervention is concluded by inviting responses from group members.

Statements from group members, at this point, usually range from personal anxieties to generally shared anxieties concerning lack of direction. As much as is possible, all the major sources of anxiety should be discussed, with shared concerns being emphasized wherever they exist. This discussion may serve to bring group members closer together and will provide the groundwork for future sharing and disclosure. These statements will undoubtedly bring up concerns centering around disclosure, trust, and authority, and these concerns will offer fruitful sources of future group direction. This set of interventions is a significant variation of Critical Incident B-9.

Intervention Outcome

This intervention is designed to allow group members to experience the anxiety-eliciting silences that usually emerge in groups. In addition to the intervention discussed above, the group leader may also utilize a structural intervention that underscores the fears and anxieties of all members. In exploring the various anxiety-based concerns of the group, the group leader is in an excellent position to emphasize the issue of disclosure—or trust or authority—in considerable detail. The group leader can "shape" the discussion into areas that are productive for all members. He might further narrow the issue of authority by asking, "Whose authority in this group causes some anxiety?" and thus gradually lead the group toward a more interpersonal sharing level.

Critical Incident B-11: Who Is Responsible?

Theme Topics: Goal Ambiguity and Diffuse Anxiety
Members' Search for Position/Definition:
Primary Group Transferences/
Countertransferences

Context of Incident

This critical incident occurs during the early phases of group growth. The climate is one of frustration because of consistent refusals on the part of the leader to assume responsibility for group decisions. As various topics and plans are discussed and dropped, or only partially pursued, one aggressive group member turns to the group leader.

Event Preceding Choice Point

Ursula: "I'm getting frustrated. I thought you were supposed to tell us what to do—otherwise how can we know what to do? We're getting nowhere this way!"

The group turns to observe the leader's reaction.

Choice Point

During this stage of the group, certain members may begin to express their frustration by directing hostile statements toward the group leader. It is at this point that the leader will have to decide (a) whether one member is reflecting the feeling of the group or (b) whether this member is responding as an individual whose life style is one of aggressive confrontation, reflecting personal (and not group) needs.

The intervention chosen will depend on the decision made by the leader as to the underlying issue: group frustration/anxiety or individual hostility.

Here, Ursula is regarded as reflecting the feelings of the group for the leader. As such, the issues involved deal with group counterdependency, the role of authority, membership responsibility, and the establishment of goals. The leader should also keep in mind that this may be an individual who is expressing aggressive counterdependent behavior as a beginning challenge to group leadership. Since it is acknowledged that motives behind a statement may be mixed (or even unknown to the sender), the leader should respond with a minimally threatening intervention directed at the primary motive judged to be operating in the member or group.

What would you do at this point? Give rationale.

Suggested Intervention

Group Leader: "I certainly sense your frustration and anger at me, Ursula. I'm sure this isn't the first time you've been angry and it'll probably happen again." (Individual level, experiential type, medium intensity.) "There are some good reasons for this, because ordinarily when you come into a group you have certain expectations concerning authority and leadership. We automatically assume that leaders will lead and will be authoritative. That relieves us somewhat, because then we don't have to confront ourselves when we work together; someone else is doing it for the entire group. I think this is what is happening now." (A shift to group level, conceptual type, low intensity.) "You are angry at me, Ursula, because apparently I haven't lived up to an expectation that you brought in from the outside." (A movement back to individual level, experiential type, medium intensity.)

The leader continues: "There are probably a number of other people who have similar expectations, so I don't think you are alone in this. The point is that authority is one of the most important issues that we're going to have to deal with. If you notice, even with the little time we've been together, you've responded to me in one of two ways: either you've wanted to lean on me—be dependent—by asking me to tell you what to do, or you have attacked me when I haven't 'come across.' Maybe some other members would like to comment on this." (Group level, conceptual type, medium intensity.) The leader concludes by turning the process back to the group for discussion and analysis.

Intervention Outcome

This intervention may legitimize the genuine expression of feelings in the group, whether toward the leader or between group members. In addition, certain issues of leadership, authority, and expected roles are emphasized as underlying factors in the just-finished process. This may lead to further exploration in areas that would facilitate group and individual expression. It is often helpful to clarify the underlying feelings by using an optional structural intervention, e.g., tossing a pillow or paper cup to the member and asking him to respond to it in any way he feels like doing, as if it were the leader.

Optional Structural Intervention

8. Fantasy in Association, p. 219

Critical Incident B-12: Counterdependency

*Theme Topics: **Goal Ambiguity and Diffuse Anxiety***
*   **Members' Search for Position/Definition:***
*   **Primary Group Transferences/***
*   **Countertransferences***

Context of Incident

This event occurs during the beginning phase of group life. The climate of the group is one of counterdependency, testing the limits of the leader and involving an attempt to develop a consensus around group goals. The entire group has just spent a great deal of time engaged in a heated discussion about whether you are a group leader, a group member, or something else. During this entire time, you, as a group leader, have remained a quiet observer of the discussion. You have noted that the group has talked about you and around you as if you were not there.

Event Preceding Choice Point

The entire group now seems on the verge of making a decision either to include or to exclude you, to assign you a particular role or to decide what direction the group should follow. The group is now in the process of voting or taking a consensus.

Victor: "O.K. Let's see a show of hands. All for the proposal, raise your hands . . . " A vote has now been taken.

Choice Point

There are a number of issues involved here. One is the group vs. the leader or the dependency/counterdependency issue. Another is the means of evading personal confrontation with the authority problem. Another issue focuses on the underlying needs that prompt this particular incident, such as individual bids for power and control of the group. The issue the leader chooses to underscore should be the most obvious motivating factor. Following this observation, the less central underlying issues should also be touched upon.

What would you do at this point? Give rationale.

Suggested Intervention

Almost invariably, for this type of critical incident the leader's intervention begins on an experiential note at the group level.

Group Leader: "For the last thirty minutes you have been talking about how to deal with authority in the group. In other words, how to deal with me." (Group level, conceptual type, medium intensity.) This intervention conceptualizes the problem of authority but identifies it specifically in terms of a personal reference in the group.)

The leader continues: "The entire time this has been going on, you've been talking about me as if I were somehow out of the group without confronting me directly." (A continuation of identifying the process.) "The pattern in our group seems to be either uncritical acceptance or equally uncritical rejection. Neither of these seems very satisfying, and yet we can't seem to stop swinging back and forth between them. The problem of authority is a reality in this group, and I can't magically legislate away both the issues and problems of authority. What I can do is try to work as openly as I can in confronting you with what I see happening, including my own involvement in it, so we can work on the authority problems directly." (Group level, conceptual/experiential type, medium intensity.) This leader response continues to be on the conceptual level but related to a personal involvement in the group issue, providing the group with an opportunity to respond.

Another intervention at a higher intensity level:

Group Leader: "If the group has agreed not to treat me as a member or not to treat me as an authority, I recognize the decision you made. But it is an unreal one. I don't feel bound by it since I wasn't included in the discussion or the outcome." (Group level, experiential type, high intensity.)

This type of intervention, in contrast to the preceding one, usually serves to heighten the conflict between members and leader and may lead to direct personal encounter with one or more members. This usually takes the form of members requesting that the leader "define his role" or "tell us what to do." These responses again lead back to authority and control issues.

This critical incident is a prototype, since groups will typically try to "vote in or out" certain goals (or even the leader) without exploring how they reached a decision or what their underlying motivations are.

Intervention Outcome

The first intervention demonstrates how a group member or leader can be a participant in an ongoing group process and yet be an observer of that process at the same time. It also introduces the complex issue of the relationship between the leader and group members. What, exactly, is the leader's role?

Is he a group member or not? Does he vote, and, if so, how much weight does he carry in group decision making? Can he be assigned duties or relegated to a certain position inside or outside the group? What are the general stereotypes of relating to authority, and can creative risk taking improve upon these relationships? Questions such as these serve to help the group investigate not only the specific problems involved, but their more general applicability to larger groups.

The second intervention is often utilized when the leader wishes to "sharpen up" the issues involved in the conflict. It is especially useful when the members are only partially involved in the discussion leading to a decision involving the leader or some ambiguous group goal. In these instances, a high-intensity intervention increases the tension and tends to polarize the group members, thereby increasing their involvement. It should be recognized that high-intensity interventions may result in immediate personal encounters on a one-to-one basis, which the leader must be prepared to handle.

Critical Incident B-13:
If You're the Leader, Lead

Theme Topic: Members' Search for Position/Definition:
Primary Group Transferences/
Countertransferences

Context of Incident

During the early group stages, group members bring with them certain fixed ideas about the proper behavior for anyone designated as a group leader. If the group leader does not fulfill these expectations, the members may seek to clarify the leader's position by questioning his role and function. Some members may react with frustration and direct anger toward the leader. Others may withdraw and become passive. The climate of this critical incident is identified by uncertainty, hostility, and a lack of direction. It might occur following a series of attempts, on the part of group members, to confront the group leader and force him into a certain prescribed role.

Event Preceding Choice Point

Wilma: "My image of you has really changed. You keep saying you're a resource person, but I want to know whether you're a leader or not! Just what do you see as your role or place in the group—if *any!*"

Choice Point

At the surface level, this request for information is an attempt to determine what it is that you, the leader, might want the group to do. However, it is apparent from the member's posture, intensity, and tone of voice that she is expressing more than a simple request. In this instance, there is implied anger, counterdependency, and criticism toward the leader for not fulfilling "good leadership behavior." If the leader is reasonably sure that a number of messages are being communicated, these should be answered or deferred, depending on the intention. The above incident may be the beginning of a low-level confrontation between member and leader and may well provide a prototype for future interpersonal encounters. Encounters often begin in this form, with an implied criticism of role or function. Later, an encounter may be directed toward personal idiosyncracies or personality traits. The leader may also sense that primary group transferences in the form of unrealistic emotions may be operating.

What would you do at this point? Give rationale.

Suggested Intervention

Group Leader: "That's a good question, Wilma, but I don't think it's a neutral question—that is, one without some sense of feeling. It's more than a request for me to define my position, because I certainly felt some anger in it. Probably you're spending a good deal of your time trying to figure out just what in the devil I'm supposed to be doing. And why I'm not doing the same thing each time. And I can buy that. The point is that you have a certain expectation about leadership, that it ought to be consistent, that I should spell out in detail what is to be done and how, that I establish the norms for what we will or will not do, that I somehow meet the expectations of your ideas of leadership brought in here from other groups. I certainly see myself as both a member and a resource person, wherever I can be helpful in those ways—perhaps by using my own behavior as a model and as a way of representing membership in the group. I'm going to try to be a catalyst in getting everyone to work out his own questions of membership and leadership." (Individual level, experiential/conceptual type, medium intensity.) Although at the individual level, this intervention is expressed in such a manner that it has general applicability.

Intervention Outcome

This intervention was designed to establish the relevancy of membership/authority issues, as well as the recognition of emotions emerging from frustrated expectancies. This intervention should provide the opening for an investigation of attitudes toward authority, the right of members to assume responsibility for their direction, and the possibility of membership becoming a form of participative leadership.

The leader's statement may appear to be ambiguous, but it reflects the recognition and legitimacy of group feelings and an understanding that problems between member and leader are based on preconceived ideas about proper role behaviors. The relevance of such stereotypes and generalizations is less important than an understanding of their origins and applicability—or lack of it—to this emerging group. There are those group members who at this point may literally "demand" a concrete answer, a step-by-step answer. This critical incident often leads to a sharpening of the authority issue, and it may be particularly threatening to the beginning group leader.

Optional Structural Intervention

9. What Is My Place?, p. 221

Critical Incident B-14: Making Decisions

Theme Topic: Members' Search for Position/Definition:
Primary Group Transferences/
Countertransferences

Context of Incident

This critical incident usually emerges as the group attempts to make decisions on its own. Typically, these decisions are tentative and heavily weighted toward areas that members feel would be "approved" by the group leader. Although the event occurs more often during the early stages, it may sometimes be seen in the middle stages. The climate of the group is such that the more aggressive group members begin seeking concrete rules to follow.

Event Preceding Choice Point

The group is involved in a discussion, attempting to reach a solution to a group problem.

Xavier (turning to the group leader): "As a resource person, tell me, is consensus, or a majority, or what, absolutely necessary for a decision?"

Yolanda: "Yeah, and after we make our decision, I'd like to know if you agree with it or go along with it!"

The group now sits silently waiting for your response, apparently in agreement with these two members.

Choice Point

On the surface, this critical incident involves a straightforward request for information. However, there may be more substantive issues that deserve recognition. Closer inspection of this critical incident during this stage of group life reveals underlying attitudes toward leadership and authority. As such, this intervention involves dependency or counterdependency in connection with making decisions. It also involves a "control" variable as a major component of the interest and concern of group members. Some members may begin trying to establish a position in the group by their emotional statements toward the leader.

What would you do at this point? Give rationale.

Suggested Intervention

Group Leader: "The question you're asking me has several parts to it. I think at one level you're asking me to give some support to a particular way—a specific way—the group wants to work. For example, taking a vote. But you're also asking something else, i.e., whether or not it will be good for the group to develop one particular way of making decisions, such as consensus or taking a vote." (Group level, conceptual type, low intensity.) The group leader reiterates the event to provide a framework and identifies at least one surface issue and one underlying issue as a source of legitimate concern.

He continues: "I think the question for me, then, is not whether voting is better by majority or plurality or consensus or any other means, but rather how the group members relate to one another in trying to come to grips with the problem. And certainly that is a process question—a question of the way we work (or don't work) together. Perhaps the biggest issue is 'How do we decide to make our decision?' The tendency, so far, has seemed to be that our group swings from one extreme to the other. That is, you either look to me as some kind of authority who can approve or disapprove or you want to do things by yourself and reject me completely. I seem to hear this coming up again and again, and I can't decide that for you. We're all going to have to work on it. I feel that the process of working it through—and the understanding of that process—is every bit as important as the actual decision." (Group/individual level, conceptual/experiential type, medium intensity.)

This intervention involves the group leader's individual feelings as well as their importance in the overall group process.

Intervention Outcome

The intervention attempts to identify certain issues that are crucial to the development of the group as a functioning unit, capable of participating in and observing its own growth. The suggested intervention is designed to encourage the exploration and discussion of authority relationships, the group decision-making process, and the interaction of both as an influence on groups. When these problems have been discussed to everyone's satisfaction, it is often profitable to evaluate these learnings by transferring them to other "real life" groups, with the use of concrete examples such as members' own difficulties or hindrances in making decisions or their experiences of being left out of decision making.

Optional Structural Intervention

10. The NASA Exercise, p. 223

Critical Incident B-15: Leader or Member?

***Theme Topic: Members' Search For Position/Definition:
Primary Group Transferences/
Countertransferences***

Context of Incident

This critical incident seems to be a sophisticated way to ask the leader, "Are you a member or not?" It centers around membership and norm issues as they apply to the concept of equality. This situation typically occurs after several members have discussed personal issues and expect the group leader to do the same.

Event Preceding Choice Point

Zach: "I feel that I know something about everybody in the group except the leader. I would like to hear from him."

Arlette: "I agree. I'd like to know him personally, what bugs him, what gets him upset, and so forth."

Betsy: "Well, maybe he's not supposed to tell us."

Chet: "Yeah. But I still feel he could say something."

Choice Point

There is usually a brief silence in which the leader has the choice to respond or not to respond. If he responds, he must consider the issues to which he will address himself. The surface issue is clearly what, or how much, the leader should disclose about himself personally. This is tantamount to being seduced into membership, but at times it may serve a purpose. The underlying issue is the norms of membership and position and how these apply to the leader. The authority issue is also involved, since the members are making a bid to establish equality with the leader. If the leader responds at this latter level, he will answer the issues *and* set a good model for the group members by recognizing that members are seeking to define their position in relation to the leader.

What would you do at this point? Give rationale.

Suggested Intervention

Group Leader: "Well, I'd like to share with you a little bit of what I'm feeling right now." (Group level, experiential type, low intensity.) This response answers in part what the group has requested and yet allows the leader to decide to which issues he will respond. "I do feel somewhat tempted to go along with you; I guess I could share some things with you, and some of those things might be somewhat personal to me. On the other hand, I'm not quite sure what that might accomplish except maybe a feeling that we could be one big, happy family, and I would be one of you and everything would be kind of 'peaches and cream.' I don't see anything wrong with that, and it does hold a great deal of temptation for me, but I do feel that there are some responsibilities that are very difficult for me to relinquish." (Group level, conceptual type, low intensity.) This response should help explain some of the expectancies that may have arisen from the leader's earlier comments.

"One responsibility is trying to participate in what is going on as much as possible so that I can grow, because I feel that any group that intends to move anywhere tends to take the leader along with it—sometimes with the leader initiating, sometimes with the group initiating—but with both growing from mutually enhancing experiences. I feel a certain responsibility to try to remain as objective as I can and yet as involved as possible in what's going on. And so I can't help but try to question why you want me to do this. On one hand you seem to be saying, 'Hey, you can be one of us,' and on the other, like an old Pogo comic strip, you are saying, 'We have met the enemy and they is us!' This seems to fit pretty well, too, because if the group absorbs me, perhaps I won't be as much of a threat, and we won't be as much of a threat to each other. But I'm not sure that would serve the purpose of growth, and I think that is what we are here to do—to grow." (Group level, conceptual type, medium intensity.)

Intervention Outcome

This type of "semipersonal" leader disclosure will probably have several effects. For one, the group will see that the leader can become involved if he chooses and yet remain free to determine his own role in the group. Secondly, the group will be helped to become aware of the pressure it can exert and to direct it to a useful group-oriented goal. Thirdly, by approaching a salient issue (mutual threat) through an analysis of the discrepancy between surface and underlying issues, the group will not have the feeling of being punished.

An optional structural intervention may be utilized at this point to illustrate how each member looks to every other member, as well as to the leader.

Optional Structural Intervention

8. Fantasy in Association, p. 219

Critical Incident B-16: Dealing with Feelings

Theme Topics: Members' Search for Position/Definition:
Primary Group Transferences/
Countertransferences
Sharpened Affects and Anxieties:
Increased Defensiveness

Context of Incident

During the early phase and through the middle phase of group development, the climate of this group is task oriented, somewhat rigid, and inclined to ignore emotional issues when they arise. As group leader, you have repeatedly called the group's attention to events it has ignored as being perhaps too threatening. One of the group members, who is rigid and formalistic, sits glaring at you as you finish another brief intervention. Finally he speaks directly to you in a loud, authoritative voice that is filled with anger and accusation.

Event Preceding Choice Point

Dale: "I've been watching you, and it seems to me that you're deliberately trying to stir everyone up and get us angry or emotional. I think you're doing it on purpose and I want to know why! I don't like it. I don't think our emotions have anything to do with the task we are discussing here. Every time we try to make a decision, we get sidetracked on some emotional thing and you seem to encourage it!"

The group falls silent, waiting for your response.

Choice Point

There may be several issues involved in this important critical incident. Whether the issues are surface issues or underlying issues depends on circumstances. For example, the surface issue may be a simple request for a clarification and a statement of the position that the leader is taking, with no other motive. In this instance, both the surface and underlying issues coincide. However, the surface issue may disguise a challenge to authority and a bid for position and control on the part of the group member, a reflection of a personal dislike of the group leader, a feeling of sharpened anxiety and increased defensiveness concerning the free expression of emotion, a bias on the part of the group member that a man does not show emotion in front of others, or any combination of the above. The response to this critical incident, therefore, will vary depending upon the impact that is desired. The suggested intervention touches briefly on all the above, allowing the group leader to selectively emphasize those issues he believes to be of importance to the group.

What would you do at this point? Give rationale.

Suggested Intervention

An intervention involving a direct encounter between a group member and the group leader almost invariably begins at the personal level on a one-to-one basis. Except under certain unusual circumstances, it would be a mistake to leave it at this level, since the implications of this encounter usually have profound effects upon the future of the group. The discipline of the group leader should not only prevent this intervention from becoming a limited personal encounter but should also transform it into an issue that has relevance to all members and to the group as a whole. This kind of intervention is more effective if it begins as an experiential type of low intensity. A high-intensity intervention would seem to reflect a defensiveness that is not necessary at this point.

Group Leader: "I certainly hear what you're asking, Dale, and at the same time I'm getting a gut feeling that you're pretty angry—perhaps at me. Am I right? If you're asking that we as a group or even that I personally ignore the emotional and maintenance problems, I don't feel we could, even if we wanted to. The very fact that there is a good deal of anger in your statement seems to point up this fact." (Individual level, experiential type, medium intensity.) The leader gradually identifies the question and points out its importance, first to the group and then back to Dale as a member of that group.

"The group that can effectively blend both task and maintenance (or emotional issues) to achieve any given goal seems, to me, to be the best kind of functioning group. It is precisely because we have avoided dealing with emotional issues that we have been blocked from becoming an effective task group." (Group level, conceptual type, medium intensity.) "This leads me to wonder what standards or norms we have established, at least implicitly, concerning the expression of emotion." (Group level, conceptual type, low intensity.)

The leader identifies this issue as one of importance for the entire group, a necessary component of movement and growth. His response points out a very important related area—values and norms—as another possibility for group concern. This in turn might yield statements from the group concerning disclosure, trust, support, confidence, and risk taking. Selective reinforcement at this point, such as the following question by the group leader, might well move the group into other important areas.

Group Leader: "I wonder how the rest of you feel right now, about Dale's statements and about my observations?" (Group level, experiential type, low intensity.) This comment returns the discussion to the group for analysis.

Intervention Outcome

This intervention was designed to recognize and legitimize the expression of emotion by group members. It also provides a model for a confrontation process. If this intervention were to remain at a high-intensity level, it might well inhibit other members from engaging in direct expressions of anger and prevent any attempts at conflict resolution. Opening up the issue in a way that involves group members as resources may make the applicability of general concepts and skills become apparent and thus make them utilized by the group.

In order to illustrate the importance and relevance of emotional responses to others—particularly how these responses determine a large part of our behavior—the leader may decide to use an optional structural intervention as a focus for the discussion of emotions.

Optional Structural Intervention

11. Eyeballing, p. 228

Critical Incident B-17:
Confronting Resistance

Theme Topic: Members' Search for Position/Definition:
Primary Group Transferences/
Countertransferences

Context of Incident

At some point during the early stages of group life, there may be several individuals who will strongly resist the interventions and suggestions for activities on the part of the group leader. Such a counterdependent individual may have initiated this resistance from the very first session, or he may just recently have started feeling comfortable enough to confront the leader. Often, this member will have exhibited either a lack of interest or passive-aggressive behavior toward much of the group activity in previous sessions.

Event Preceding Choice Point

The group leader has made a suggestion for an activity designed to draw all members closer together through a sharing dyad. (See Critical Incident B-1 and B-3.) The exact nature of the activity, however, is irrelevant to the following process of counterdependency.

Ernie: "Do you really think that will do any good at all at this time? I don't know. I just don't feel like I got much out of the last dyad. Do you really think we're going to get anything out of this? What's it going to do for us?"

The group is now waiting for the leader's response.

Choice Point

This critical incident could be treated, at the surface level, as a genuine request for information, a reflection of the questions other group members might have at this point about structural interventions. On another level, however, the group leader should recognize and respond to the underlying issues of counterdependency, opposing life styles, confrontation with authority, and membership responsibilities.

What would you do at this point? Give rationale.

Suggested Intervention

Group Leader: "Look, Ernie, I can fairly quickly answer the first part. Obviously, I wouldn't have suggested it if I hadn't thought there was some potential for group growth. But I can't guarantee it. It depends. It depends on the involvement and commitment of people like yourself. And I think that's crucial. Up to now you have been relatively uninvolved. And that's all right, because I think every individual has to make his choice. And yet, what does it mean in terms of people being able to help one another? I translated your statement to say 'What a dumb thing to do! You can't really believe that's going to help!' It occurs to me that you're angry and irritated. Right? I've been trying to communicate with you and you've appeared relatively inactive and angry. I need to know what's going on between you and the group, but most importantly between you and me. O.K., I've done some sharing with you. Will you share your thoughts and feelings with me?" (Individual level, experiential type, medium intensity.)

The intervention both acknowledges the legitimacy of Ernie's question and deals with the deeper, underlying, and implicit issues previously discussed. If carried through successfully, it should benefit the individual member and provide modeling behavior for the constructive resolution of conflict for the other group members. The last statement by the group leader encourages the group member to share the reasons for his counterdependent behavior. There are a number of points here that the group leader and member might wish to pursue. The direction taken will depend largely on the interaction between the theoretical orientation of the leader and his particular interaction style.

Intervention Outcome

It is obvious that the above intervention response involves considerable risk taking on the part of the leader. It is consequently necessary for him to exercise some judgment in choosing whether to confront the individual. His response to the member could well be at the surface level, but this would merely postpone an inevitable confrontation. The same question asked by a very involved but momentarily confused group member would be answered quite differently—as a legitimate request for information and clarification. The depth of confrontation chosen will largely depend on the experience of the group leader as well as his judgment of the situation.

Critical Incident B-18: Testing the Limits

Theme Topic: Members' Search for Position/Definition:
Primary Group Transferences/
Countertransferences

Context of Incident

This incident occurs during the early to middle phases of group life. Counterdependency and a desire to test the limits of the group leader's position form the climate of the event.

As group leader, you have been having direct one-to-one encounters with two particularly "irritating and rigid" group members. You have just finished giving constructive feedback to a particularly frustrated and blocked member and have even commented on these feelings. Following your comments, there is a moment of silence; then one of the other group members, who has been quite hostile in the past and tends to assert himself in an authoritarian manner, turns and speaks directly to you with a smirk on his face.

Event Preceding Choice Point

Flynn: "It looks to me like you are pretty angry. Are you—are you mad at him?" He looks at you expectantly, waiting for you to answer.

Choice Point

The issues involved in this complex incident are concerned with authority and dependency, the struggle for leadership, the expression of anger, and the role of the leader and his position in the group. In addition, there is the issue of personal, one-to-one confrontation. The competent group leader must learn to respond selectively to those issues that are most salient and productive for the group. Certain group members, jockeying for power or position in the group, will often watch for signs of human frailty, shortcomings, or frustrations that they can identify and pointedly comment on.

What would you do at this point? Give rationale.

Suggested Intervention

Group Leader: "You're right, Flynn. I was frustrated and irritated when I responded to Ernie." (Individual level, experiental type, high intensity.)

This simple statement of fact might well be the leader's first choice and would allow the group to use the honest expression of feeling as a model in an attempt to deal with this matter. Another intervention strategy exposing the feelings and issues involved:

Group Leader: "Flynn, let me share a couple of feelings with you. One has to do with Ernie, about whom you were asking, and one has to do with you. As far as Ernie is concerned, you're right in noting that I was frustrated and angry with him. On the other hand, I have felt you being angry with me, and in one way or another you've expressed this hostility—but always indirectly. A case in point is here and now, expressing your feelings clearly but indirectly by encouraging a kind of battle between me and Ernie—like being a spectator and watching two gladiators in the arena. Now, I'd like to ask you the same question. Are you angry and can you level with me? Somehow I feel this may be a crucial issue involving your attempt to control the situation, control me, deal with authority, and express anger, all in one package. All of these are important in their consequences for the group, ranging from how we express ourselves to how we struggle for control and membership. Could you give me some feedback on this, Flynn? And could the rest of you help as you see appropriate?" (A movement from individual level, experiential type, high intensity, to group level in order to include issues of general concern, inviting other members' observations and services as resources.)

Intervention Outcome

This intervention serves two basic purposes. First, it cuts through the surface statements of one member and goes directly to the underlying, motivating issue. Secondly, it attempts to legitimize the direct handling of conflict in a productive manner by inviting the resources of the group in the form of feedback. Future conflicts between group members or between group members and the leader will be able to profit from this situation; in addition, members will hesitate less in trying to deal with important conflicts as they arise. The group leader has touched on the issues of control, authority, and hostility to sensitize the group members to the many possible motivating factors behind this conflict encounter. The issue the leader then chooses to emphasize is thus placed in a context of overall group process.

Critical Incident B-19: Confronting the Leader

Theme Topic: Members' Search for Position/Definition:
Primary Group Transferences/
Countertransferences

Context of Incident

This critical incident involves leadership and authority issues with a particular focus on strong feelings of counterdependency. Often hostility toward
the leader is also expressed, with special attention to his inconsistent or
ambiguous role in the group. It typically follows an intervention in which the
leader has pointed out some reality factors that would make a suggested
group proposal impractical to carry out. One of the members of the group
then confronts the leader.

Event Preceding Choice Point

Georgia: "You shoot down every idea that anyone comes up with. And I hate
the way you switch roles: sometimes you're a member like the rest of us and
sometimes a leader who tells us what to do and sometimes an observer who
just sits and watches. Well" (in a louder voice), *"you can't be all of those!"*

Choice Point

The surface issue is the role of the leader and one member's reaction to this
ambiguous role. Issues also present are authority relations, norms of group
membership, members searching for position and definition, and the expression of hostility in general. Another issue in this incident is that of group
growth and the process by which a group gets to the point where authority
can be recognized and challenged. Georgia could be expressing countertransference as part of the surface issue of the group's "authority problem."

66

What would you do at this point? Give rationale.

Suggested Intervention

Group Leader: "Georgia, I do want to acknowledge your feelings. I know that you are angry with me. I don't want to run away from it, but I would like to have an opportunity now to comment on what is going on, especially since this has happened before." (Individual level, experiential type, low intensity.) This intervention answers the emotional attitude of the group member and facilitates a "mind set" of the group for the conceptual intervention to follow.

"Several times, one of you—you, Dale, or Herb, or Arlette, and a few others—would throw down a gauntlet, challenge me, or in some way attempt to control my behavior in such a way that no matter what I did, I would lose. You quite literally put me in a 'no win' situation. Let me tell you what I mean."

Herb: "No, we don't. You set the situation up."

Arlette: "Yeah. You're switching roles again."

Group Leader: "Okay. Give me a chance to finish and then you can come back in any way that makes sense to you." (Individual level, experiential type, medium intensity.) The leader answers Arlette's immediate comment and gives other members an "in" to respond later.

"What I was trying to say is that some of you have put me in a double bind. If I don't say anything I'm either intimidated or deceitful. If I answer you, I can only fight with you or capitulate. Whether I fight you and win or capitulate and lose, you have succeeded in getting me to respond in ways that you want. You've gotten me into *your* definition of my role. If I refuse to do any of these, you threaten to kick me out of the group. And it all seems to create a high tension 'pocket,' while the rest of the group backs off to see what is going to happen—to see whether I take the bait or not." (Group level, experiential type, high intensity.) This intervention is aimed at generating responses that could lead to further clarification of the dynamics.

"What I have chosen to do now is to try to explain at some length what I see happening. I'm not going to accept any of the alternatives you gave me. I'm not going to try them. In fact, I'm going to try not to use them. Instead, I'll try to explain what I see happening and try to discuss with you, as reasonably as we can, some of the dynamics underlying our experiences. I think that if you really wanted to make this a learning situation, you would want to discuss with me, with my help and the help of others, some of the personal implications for your new role in all of this, and I would like to talk to you. And I don't mean punitively, either; but about your feelings, how you feel about me, and why. About why I am seen as someone to be feared, somebody to get angry with. It would be useful for me and for Herb and Arlette and the others.

"If you're willing, what I am proposing is that we pick up on this and talk about our feelings and invite others to come in and be consultants to us. It's a kind of experiment we could do if we are really interested in gaining further understanding." (Group level, conceptual type, medium intensity.)

Intervention Outcome

If the member agrees and gets into a personal discussion with the leader, work on leadership issues can proceed, while establishing a model for later encounters and a system or norm for dealing with this type of conflict. Or Georgia may say, "I don't see what we're going to get out of it, but I'll go along." Although she is still defending herself against losing, she is willing to attempt to learn—a healthy situation. In either of these two situations, the group and the leader can explore, in a very personal way and supportive manner, the member's feeling toward the leader.

Frequently, a typical response is of another nature and constitutes another challenge, e.g., "I think you're manipulating again." The feeling is that after the amount of time already spent and the issues that have been brought up, the group would truly lose if the issue were dropped at this point. Here, the leader might well raise the intensity to high, shifting from a request for interaction to interpret-reinterpret, and thus encounter the group member on a one-to-one basis.

Group Leader: "Georgia, what you're doing now is the same thing as before. You're making it impossible for me to work with you in any way other than beating you over the head or letting you do the same to me. I will not be controlled by you. I don't know how any of the others in our group feel, but I am not going to play a game with you right now. I want us to help each other. I do. But I am not going to choose one of those three choices: to get the hell out of the group, to beat the hell out of you, or to get stomped on. That's what I believe you're doing. Do you see that you're doing that? It's the same thing you did before. When are you going to try to take a step in the direction of finding out more about it? Maybe the others can help. If you keep doing this and you don't penetrate beyond this level of uncritical rejection of me, then I think you're doing a disservice to yourself.

"We have talked about the problem of authority before, Georgia, and how it involves both overdependence, which at times you have experienced, and counterdependence. People vacillate from intense feelings of overdependence to intense counterdependence. And we now seem to be, in the swing of the pendulum, at the point of counterdependence. I think it is important that we stop and look at it. I know it provokes anxiety, and I know you're angry. But will you work with me on it?" (Individual level, experiential type, high intensity.) This type of exchange is usually enough to get the member into the arena so that the personal issues can be worked.

This is not an easy critical incident to face and it may demand a great deal of control and discipline on the part of the group leader. Direct encounters of critical hostility toward the leader place demands on him that can be successfully handled only through experience and a sense of commitment to seeing the process through to the end.

Critical Incident B-20: Expressing Anger

Theme Topic: Members' Search for Position/Definition: Primary Group Transferences/ Countertransferences

Context of Incident

This critical incident occurs during the early to middle stages of group life and usually emerges when one or more members express a great deal of anger toward the group leader. This may be due to an especially aggressive member, who seeks and enjoys interpersonal conflict and encounter. At other times, this emerging hostility may be due to a disagreement with procedural issues or frustration over the inability to resolve a group problem. Regardless of the precipitating cause, this is likely to be a rather high-intensity encounter. The climate of the group may become especially tense and strained.

Event Preceding Choice Point

The leader has just presented his observation that the group has avoided dealing with certain issues.

Ivan: "I think you are doing what you accuse us of doing, fabricating one of those self-fulfilling prophecies!"

This remark is followed by laughter and comments among some of the group members, especially the more hostile ones.

Choice Point

This incident involves several issues. On one level it deals with a group member's accusatory statement directed toward the group leader. At another level it may be a bid for leadership and authority, especially as revealed in counterdependent activity involving control issues. It may be an attempt to take over directional guidance of the group. Underlying anger between the leader and a member may often emerge as seemingly objective statements that offer a focal point for the conflict. This critical incident thus involves an interpersonal conflict surfacing as a minor issue.

What would you do at this point? Give rationale.

Suggested Intervention

The group leader might choose to remain silent or defend his previous intervention or seek the real reasons for the anger. This is not to assume that there is never a legitimate disagreement that is just that—a surface disagreement. The point is that the judgment of the leader is a necessary factor in choosing the appropriate response, whether simple or complex.

Group Leader: "I certainly hear the anger in your voice, Ivan." (Individual level, experiential type, medium intensity.) This response is a direct recognition of the feelings involved.

"Let me ask you a couple of questions, all right? When you made that comment, regardless of whether it's true—we can test that out in a moment with the group—were you interested in helping me?" (Individual level, experiential type, medium intensity.) The purpose at this point is to encourage Ivan to explore the roots of his anger.

Ivan: "No, I just wanted to make an observation. You encourage us to express our feelings, but when I'm angry and want to express my feelings, I don't stop to think 'Am I going to help so-and-so?' I want to help myself!"

Group Leader: "I know. That's what I was observing. Are you very angry at me?"

Ivan: "Yeah! I'm angry for the group and it bothers me. This is a nice group of people and . . . "

Group Leader: "I feel it's a cop-out when you say you're angry only for the group. I believe that you're angry for yourself. Are you angry for yourself? You see, you clobber me personally. O.K., but then you retreat behind the cover of the group. And that makes me wonder. So I'm respecting your anger and giving you what I think is a good deal of concern. So level with me—why are you angry and who am I to make you angry?" (An intervention that continues the intensity of the encounter and does not allow the member to retreat back into the group or to defend himself as speaking for the group—individual level, experiential type, high intensity.)

Ivan: "Well, you act pompous—like my father. Do you know what he does? Sometimes he comes into the room and tells me to go somewhere else, and do you know what I do? I ignore him. Earlier today when you said something, I stayed here, but I just turned off and decided not to say anything until now—when you got me so angry I had to say something!"

Group Leader: "I can buy that much more. I really can—it comes through clear. Do you want to stay with this for a few minutes?" (Individual level, experiential type, low intensity.) "I think we're at a point now where it's pretty important to pursue this, and it can serve a number of purposes for us. If it comes up with you tomorrow, Paulette, or the next day with you, John, what would you like to see done to help in that situation? I guess the question now is how we can all help. How can this situation help us to learn good ways of handling other situations?" (Group level, experiential/conceptual type, medium intensity.)

This intervention demonstrates that a specific situation may reflect a general learning orientation for the entire group. It also provides a model for meeting conflict, not running away, and hopefully resolving the conflict. The last statement by the group leader invites the resources of all group members to work on the problem and involve themselves in it. At this point, the group leader may proceed by inviting participant observations on the just-finished process, evaluating the interpersonal conflict, asking for group suggestions for the resolution of conflict, and discussing how the techniques of resolving conflict can be generalized to other situations.

Intervention Outcome

This particular approach offers group members an opportunity to see a model for resolving conflict. It is not the only model, and it may not even be the best model for a given individual. Consequently, other group members are urged to involve themselves in ways that would facilitate the understanding and resolution of the conflict situation. It thus ceases to be a unique phenomenon and becomes a highly potent group learning process, applicable to other situations.

Critical Incident B-21: Baiting the Leader

Theme Topic: Members' Search for Position/Definition:
Primary Group Transferences/
Countertransferences

Context of Incident

This event occurs during the early to middle phases of the group. The climate of the group is generally warm and receptive, with the exception of two members who have continued to be argumentative and negative. One of these members, John, tends to intellectualize and be hostile, having established a pattern in the group of very often fighting authority with or without an obvious reason.

You have just finished giving a complex five-minute conceptual intervention to the entire group, pointing out how this theory has relevance to what has been happening in the group here and now.

Event Preceding Choice Point

John (directly to the leader): "I don't see how what you've told us has anything to do with our group or our problem. Frankly, I feel it's much too abstract to have much value at this point and I don't much care to understand it."

The entire group falls silent, looking from the member to you.

Choice Point

A number of issues are involved at this point. One is the issue of dependency-counterdependency, or how do we allow ourselves to relate to people in authority—or those who represent authority? What position does the group take toward a hostile, "deviant" member? What personal investments are group members willing to make in order to understand the group's movement and growth? Other considerations involve the past behavior pattern of the confronting group member. Which of several intervention alternatives

74

is chosen should largely depend on the pattern that the individual has established in the past in addition to where the entire group is at this given moment. It may be that this member is making a bid for leadership, expressing specific countertransference feelings, or expressing an opposing life style.

What would you do at this point? Give rationale.

Suggested Intervention

There are three possible responses that will be considered.

Group Leader: "I wonder if anyone else has been experiencing difficulty in understanding this material or seeing its relevance for the group?" (Group level, experiential type, low intensity.)

This intervention seeks consensus and constructive feedback from the group. It also removes the one-to-one confrontation to the group level and opens it up so that other group members can give both the leader and the dissenting member appropriate feedback.

A second intervention might be used if the group leader felt John was sufficiently in touch with his own emotions to be able both to express and to examine them.

Group Leader: "I wonder why you're so angry at me, John?" (Individual level, experiential type, medium intensity.)

In this approach, little attention is paid to the content of the response, and the group leader goes directly to the affect. It should be given in an empathic and nonpunitive manner. A continuation of this type of questioning intervention may well lead to a direct one-to-one confrontation between the group leader and John.

Other group leaders may prefer a high-intensity intervention at the individual level, from the beginning, in the hope of getting quickly and directly at the source of conflict. This approach is based, of course, on the judgment that it will not "freeze" the individual into not responding or into responding in a very defensive or withdrawn manner.

Group Leader: "You know, John, you've just done what you've objected to a number of times since this group was formed. You're obviously angry, and I'm honestly getting angry, too. You state that I'm abstracting things that aren't relevant. Yet it seems that what you've been doing is a good example of using a pretext to express some very real and genuine anger. But you make it very difficult for me to respond to that anger because it's hidden behind some other words and reasons. Let's both stop being abstract right now and level with each other. I'm telling you I'm angry, so share your feelings with me so that we can try to handle this problem." (Individual level, experiential type, high intensity.)

This intervention increases the probability of a continuing series of one-to-one critical-incident statements.

At the appropriate point, the group leader can call on the group for help, thereby elevating this intervention to a group level.

Intervention Outcome

The nature of this critical incident lends it to a study of conflict and the resolution of conflict in regard to authority. A one-to-one emotional encounter will probably not terminate with the leader's final response described above. There will undoubtedly be a continuing series of statements from the group member, amplifying and extending his opposition. The task of the group leader is to explore as fully as possible the basis for this anger and opposition and then to encourage other members to enter in with their observations. It may well be that the conflict reflects the unconscious life style of the individual, or the leader may resemble a hated father or authority (the "establishment"). Whatever the reasons, and regardless of the line of conflict that is pursued, it is considered vital to utilize this critical incident as a source of involvement and growth for both the group and the individual and to pursue it until it is resolved.

Critical Incident B-22: Conflict Between Members

Theme Topic: Sharpened Affects and Anxieties: Increased Defensiveness

Context of Incident

During the late/early to early/middle stages of group development, the climate of the group becomes oriented around the avoidance of conflict, increased defensiveness, and the attempt to smooth things over and to insist on courtesy and politeness. Two group members have engaged in a number of brief skirmishes that the group has managed to ignore or divert. For some moments now, the two members have been glaring at each other.

Event Preceding Choice Point

Karl: "Lennie, I'm still mad as hell at you for criticizing every last one of my suggestions."

Lennie: "You're not by yourself, buddy. I can't get any work done with you always butting into it."

Marie (following a moment of silence): "Let's get down to specific proposals. I feel our task should be the establishment of a group agenda and then . . ." She continues the discussion, ignoring the brief interchange between Karl and Lennie.

Choice Point

The surface issue is a brief, intense personal encounter between two group members who are preventing each other from making meaningful group contributions. The surface issue is whether to attempt to pursue the group tasks or to confront the individual members with their disruptive behavior. The underlying issue is one of task vs. maintenance—determining the point at which the group can no longer meaningfully afford to ignore individual issues. This critical incident involves the first serious emergence of conflict

77

that possesses relatively high intensity of a fairly long duration. Prior to this point, "bush fighting" among members has flared up, only to die out quickly. Issues of conflict and conflict resolution among members are vital ones that determine the extent of future group growth. Consequently, this critical incident may be considered a prototype for the ability of the group to deal with other control and conflict issues.

What would you do at this point? Give rationale.

Suggested Intervention

At this point in its life, the group has no clear awareness of its responsibilities toward its members nor of the skills necessary to aid in conflict resolution. The ability or inability of the group to handle these issues should be used to discuss various "group styles" that emerge when conflict threatens the group. Thus, not only does a specific problem tend to be resolved, but the conclusions are related to broader normative issues including generalization to the larger question of conflict in other groups such as the family and business. It also helps to point out the sharpened affects and anxieties that are beginning to emerge.

Interventions at this particular phase often begin at the group level, calling attention to the sequence of events that led up to the immediate moment. Following this level, the group leader may prefer to switch to an interpersonal level, talking directly to the two antagonists and utilizing some modeling behavior to offer both of them constructive feedback. Dealing at the interpersonal level must be done skillfully, or the group leader may find himself drawn into a deepening one-to-one personal encounter. This latter type of encounter would be more appropriate in the middle or end stages and should be discouraged at this point, as potentially too disturbing. A typical response:

Group Leader: "I wonder if we might stop for a moment and consider what's been going on." (The group leader waits for the group members to respond with their feelings and perceptions.) "It seems that time and time again, I've sensed a great deal of anger between Karl and Lennie—anger that has been ignored or shunted aside by the group as a whole. I wonder if anyone else has noticed this and could comment on it." (Group level, experiential type, medium intensity.) The group leader identifies the problem and makes a request for the group to utilize its resources. After allowing the group either to identify or to fail to identify the ongoing process, the group leader continues.

"I would like us to examine what just occurred because it seems to represent some pretty important potential steps for growth." (Emphasis on group goals through a study of group process.) "That is, if one member cares enough, is involved enough to express anger and irritation and to commit himself to giving feedback to another person, then we are responsible for evaluating it as a group. Something very interesting has just occurred and I would like to share an observation with you. There was a brief, intense encounter between two group members expressing a good deal of anger. There was a moment of silence, followed by Marie and a few others suggesting another topic for the group in an entirely different area. I wish to make it clear that this is not a criticism, but a description of the process." (Group level, conceptual type, medium intensity.)

"I think this is something we all do at times; that is, to avoid pain or disturbance we choose an irrelevant topic without revealing our motive as escape. I feel it is important both to participate in the process and to recognize at the same time what is going on—to be, in short, participant observers." (A tie-in of theory with process in addition to labeling the desired group behavior.) "I wonder if we might now share what just happened between two of our group members, the reaction of the group to this, and how we might best prepare for similar events in the future." (Group level, experiential/conceptual type, medium intensity.) Other group members should be utilized as resources in order to gather observations and suggestions for the conflict resolution.

Intervention Outcome

This critical incident serves to identify a specific conflict between two or more members, to evaluate the reaction of the group to this encounter, and to attempt to establish norms for the group concerning when to pick up on the interpersonal process and when to put it aside temporarily. The leader has the option of utilizing a structural intervention designed to assist in defining and resolving the conflict.

Optional Structural Interventions

12. Releasing Anger, p. 230
13. Body Encounter, p. 232
14. Experiencing Closeness, p. 234

Critical Incident B-23: Handclasping

Theme Topic: Sharpened Affects and Anxieties: Increased Defensiveness

Context of Incident

This critical incident usually occurs in the beginning stages of group life, when individual group members attempt to pair up or subgroup, which appears to provide mutual support, protection, and a measure of security. As group leader, you have noted that several members have started out by smiling and nodding their support to statements from other group members. Very recently, this pairing has taken the form of verbal defense of certain members for each other. The group climate is one in which members are attempting to deny any negative or hostile interaction; they are attempting to achieve harmony by minimizing friction. In this incident, the specific member involved is one among many who has established the described behavior pattern. A brief hostile encounter is just beginning between two group members, when Nancy enters in.

Event Preceding Choice Point

Nancy: "Wait a minute! I agree with you, Owen. I can't understand why you, Pat, and you, Quinn, always criticize Owen. He's never hurt or criticized you! Why can't we try to get along better?"

Choice Point

While this behavior, in moderation, is natural and to be expected, the group leader must judge if it is being carried to the point where individual exploration and growth is being smothered by too much protection. This situation would indicate that the underlying process of reducing tension is being used as a reaction to conflict. The surface issue of support for another member is thus a reflection of an underlying and ongoing process. The point at which mutual support and protection prevent further growth for the group member thus becomes the choice point for an intervention.

81

What would you do at this point? Give rationale.

Suggested Intervention

Group Leader: "Let's stop a moment and take a quick look at what just happened and has been happening in here for some time. Individual members have given support to each other on a regular basis—a kind of handclasping or pairing. Sometimes this happens subtly and sometimes it is clear and crystallized, where you can almost predict that if someone jumps on Owen, Nancy is going to come in. And that's sort of a double-edged sword that has both bad and good consequences. For one thing, it's kind of nice to know you've got a Nancy ready to come in and help. But it makes it difficult for people to assume the risk, each time, of their own individual action. Other group members may see the pair as a consolidated front that intimidates them from coming in, because they know that the other ally might immediately come to the rescue. Perhaps one of the criteria for the growth of a member is the degree to which he does not consistently and excessively have to rely on the help of another to express his feelings or his position. Sometimes this might even require rejecting an apparent offer of help or support, in favor of personal self-growth. I wonder how you feel, Owen and Nancy, and the rest of you, about this?" (Begins at group level, conceptual type, low intensity, and shifts to interpersonal level, experiential type, low intensity.) This intervention is designed to initiate a discussion of the underlying issues of personal support, individual style, and member responsibility.

Optional Structural Intervention

14. Experiencing Closeness, p. 234

Critical Incident B-24: Collusion

Theme Topic: Sharpened Affects and Anxieties: Increased Defensiveness

Context of Incident

This critical incident most frequently occurs during the early stages of group life, although it is also seen during the middle stages. It usually emerges when the group climate evolves to the point where one or two group members begin to discuss highly personal issues. The freer life styles of some members require only a minimum of supportive climate before they begin to share feelings, while other, more taciturn group members may be concerned and even upset over this disclosure, since it appears to be personally threatening.

In this incident, a group member who has typically been the most spontaneous and open has just finished sharing some intensely personal thoughts and feelings with other members.

Event Preceding Choice Point

Following the member's personal statement, there is a long moment of silence, at the end of which a very conservative and visibly upset member speaks.

Rita: "Wait a minute. I'm not sure I can go along with this. I thought we agreed not to talk about personal issues!"

Choice Point

This critical incident may emerge when a group member observes that one or more other members have violated some implicit or explicit group rule. It is as if there were a tacit collusion among some group members to adhere to certain standards or rules. When these rules are broken, anxiety is sharpened and defensiveness increased. The concern is with guidelines and norm issues, as well as with inclusion and control factors. If there is a collusion—an unspoken group rule or norm—the group leader may decide to comment on this as an important group process. If there is no collusion, and the group member is responding to her own anxieties concerning disclosure, the intervention is qualitatively different. It is obvious that the implicit rule of "not talking about" certain issues, whether personal or impersonal, may have been constructed totally from the fabric of anxiety of one specific member. In such instances, the leader is dealing with a personal life style that finds the present group direction much too threatening. Any intervention must recognize both the rights of individual group members and their obligations. Sources of anxiety for members must be explored, e.g., by asking for feedback, without actively forcing anyone into a role.

At times proponents from either the liberal or conservative elements in a group may band together to enforce a rule designed to further their particular needs. This rule may have been explicitly formulated, as when a member states, "Let's agree not to talk about personal things and work on a project," or it may be implicit, as when members tacitly and pointedly avoid certain issues and areas. If allowed to continue, the implicit or explicit collusion may split a group, since sufficient attention has not been paid to differences among the members. The exact nature of the "rule" or collusion is not as important as the need for all group members to look at the underlying group process and understand its meaning for them.

What would you do at this point? Give rationale.

Suggested Intervention

The group leader may wait and remain silent, in order to evaluate the responses of other group members. If other group members disagree with Rita and a discussion of the issues results, an intervention of silence would seem to be indicated. However, if other members seem to agree with Rita, the following intervention would be appropriate.

Group Leader: "Rita, I'd like to call your attention to what you just did. It's a fairly complex thing, although on the surface it seems simple." (Individual level, conceptual type, low intensity.)

"In essence, you are calling to the attention of the group the implicit understanding that we shouldn't go into personal issues, and that's like saying we ought to have a norm or rule." (The group leader might pause at this point to emphasize the preceding thought.) "Now, the question becomes 'What if someone doesn't conform to the rules?' *Then* what do you do? Would you beat them verbally over the head? Do we exclude them from the group—deny them membership? In one sense, this question extends far beyond the limits of our group and involves such questions as 'To what extent can any group or, for that matter, nation control the behavior of its members?' 'To what extent does a member regulate and control his needs in deference to what the group or nation needs?' 'Where is the point of optimum growth for both the individual and the group?' Until we try to sort out our feelings about these issues and discover our own answers, we're not coming to grips with forces that can either impede or facilitate our movement. I can understand our anxieties and fears over this—but control through fiat or avoidance provides no opportunity for growth. Exploration of these issues, even though somewhat threatening, might be looked upon as creative risk taking." (Group level, conceptual type, medium intensity.) "Could some of you try to help clarify this further by adding your own observations?" (Group level, conceptual type, low intensity.)

Intervention Outcome

This intervention points out that the issues involved are reflections of concerns faced by every group of people, including nations, and are very realistic concerns. It is especially valuable in pointing out the "real world" concerns that are reflected, in miniature, in small-group dynamics. Understanding the dynamics involved in those issues is important in developing general concepts applicable to other group settings. Through a process of guided feedback, the entire critical incident may be an excellent introduction to the value and applicability of small-group involvement.

However, the same group member may occasionally persist in pressing for norms or rules of nonpersonal disclosure. This closely related incident and its suggested intervention might take the following form.

Rita: "Well, I kind of feel, myself, that I don't want to talk about some of these very personal things. And I thought we had all decided that we weren't going to do that kind of thing. I can understand what you mean, but I really thought we had decided that we wouldn't go into things like that. That's the way I feel about it."

Group Leader: "How do the rest of you feel about that?" (The rest of the group responds in a mixed fashion, some agreeing, some disagreeing, some undecided.) "I feel that each time this kind of thing happens, it's harder for us to talk, because there is the sense that if you don't adhere to a line, you'll get criticized. And this has some implications about how we relate and whether people feel free to grow as individuals." (Group level, conceptual type, medium intensity.)

This intervention begins by allowing the group member to receive feedback from the other group members as to his assumptions and norms for the group. Following this, a brief intervention at the group level, of a conceptual type and of medium intensity is given, pointing out the potentially destructive aspects of norms that inhibit personal expression. This does not imply that groups should not develop norms, but rather that the norms adopted should be chosen freely through a realistic and consensually based appraisal of the needs of the members.

Optional Structural Intervention

4. Introspection, p. 211

Critical Incident B-25: Bush Fighting

Theme Topic: Sharpened Affects and Anxieties:
Increased Defensiveness

Context of Incident

This critical incident takes place in a climate of conflict and fighting among group members during the latter part of the first phase of group life. When the climate of the group allows conflict and open disagreement to emerge, a certain type of "group style" appears, which is an attempt to handle friction and conflict through "sharpshooting" or sporadic "bush fighting" behavior. In this approach, there is little or no cohesive action of the group as a unit. The issues involved in the conflict may not be as important as the nature of the underlying process.

Event Preceding Choice Point

Stan: "Terry, I'm angry at you because you didn't take sides in that last statement!"

Terry: "Well, tough! I just didn't feel I had to say anything at any time in here!"

Van: "Well, that's better than some people in here. Like those three" (pointing) "that never stop trying to talk."

Choice Point

The issues involved here deal directly with the emergence of conflict among group members, as well as the underlying "bush fighting" group style that is slowly evolving. This is partially because the group has not worked out either a satisfactory method for recognizing sources of friction or a means for successfully resolving conflict. The style of reacting to conflict may tell the group leader a great deal about those issues judged to be important by individual members as well as about their capacity to resolve problems. These individual life styles usually become more sharply defined as the group progresses.

What would you do at this point? Give rationale.

Suggested Intervention

It is suggested that the group leader intervene with a conceptual input regarding group styles.

Group Leader: "One of the very interesting things you can rely on happening in a group is that the group will evolve. One significant facet of this process is the evolution in the ways in which members deal with conflict. Along with this is something called 'group style,' which is quite different, today, from what it will probably be later on in our group. Often, when people raise points of disagreement, we seem to respond in one of two ways. We ignore it, let it die quickly. That is handling conflict by burying it. Or we sometimes take pot shots at each other; that is, one or more members single out a target fairly quickly and 'let go.' This is what just occurred. The aim of this style is not to help but to oppose, since someone takes a 'shot' at you and you take a 'shot' at him, and so forth. This style generates a predictable and understandable inclination to want to respond in kind. I'd like to hear from the rest of you." (Group level, conceptual type, medium intensity.) This intervention points out the ongoing process as a descriptive statement of the present stage of the group. A high-intensity input would more likely have been interpreted by the group as criticism, freezing them up and not allowing them to explore the issues.

Intervention Outcome

The purpose of the conceptual input is to sensitize group members to both the surface and underlying issues of group process. In addition, this approach may encourage members to be more conscious of the evolutionary process of change as it occurs. It should not inhibit the free expression of conflict, but rather it should allow a more explicit understanding of group conflict. It is important to deliver the intervention carefully, in a descriptive rather than a punishing manner.

Optional Structural Interventions

4. Introspection, p. 211
13. Body Encounter, p. 232
14. Experiencing Closeness, p. 234

Critical Incident B-26: Flare-Up

Theme Topic: Sharpened Affects and Anxieties:
Increased Defensiveness

Context of Incident

This critical incident occurs during the early to middle phases of group life and illustrates how individual conflict styles begin to emerge in the group. It involves the issues of intermember "fighting" as a reaction to conflict and tension. A typical example occurs when two group members, who have previously suppressed their mutual hostility, suddenly flare up. After the two members exchange hostilities, the group, not knowing how to handle the feelings that have emerged, falls into an uneasy silence, seemingly immobilized by the confrontation.

Event Preceding Choice Point

Al: "When Barbara said that, it just made me feel angry, and made me see red."
    Barbara: "Well, Al, I couldn't care less what you think! Why don't you just shut up and keep your opinions to yourself?"
    The two continue to exchange angry looks while the group falls into an uneasy silence.

Choice Point

The surface issue is intensely hostile feelings between two group members. The most pressing underlying issue is the group's immobilization in the face of interpersonal conflict. The issue of conflict and conflict resolution is important, since the intensity of the encounter may "freeze" the group and stall further growth by intensifying affect and anxiety while members are not prepared to cope with their feelings.

What would you do at this point? Give rationale.

Suggested Intervention

Group Leader: "We've had about twenty uncomfortable seconds now, and it seems like a long time since Al and Barbara had their exchange. What's been going on is very complicated. It seems to me that it deals with how we function as individuals and how we relate to each other as group members. I'd like to take some time out and explore these with you." (Group level, conceptual type, low intensity.)

This intervention attempts to reduce the tension that has momentarily immobilized the group and to promote a freeing movement. Secondly, it attempts to give direction concerning the group's reaction to interpersonal conflict among its members.

The group leader continues: "Al and Barbara are silent. It seems as if a charge was building up for a while and then it was released very intensely. Where did it go? Has it been expressed? The tension is still there but what is its direction? Most of us, as a group, withdrew from the highly charged area as the exchange took place, as if moving away from an electrically charged fence. So, when they ended kind of abruptly, we didn't know what to do. So here we are." (Group level, experiential type, medium intensity.) This shift may get some members of the group back into the "mood" of the critical incident, to experience for themselves any feelings they could not deal with as the interchange occurred between Al and Barbara.

"Some of us may have feelings about Al, some of us may have feelings about Barbara, and some of us may have feelings about what went on between them. Al certainly is feeling certain things, as is Barbara. What do we do? How do we handle this? For one thing, I'd like to begin by asking Al and Barbara to talk to each other, to respond out loud, to think out loud, about the things that have been said to each other." (Interpersonal level, experiential type, medium intensity.) This response may help Al and Barbara become involved enough to open up more to the group.

"I know Al was taken aback when Barbara, in so many words, attacked him, and I'd personally like to know how he felt about that. And I'd like to know how Barbara felt when Al became the aggressor, which was a change in his role in this group. And some of us backed off perhaps because we were afraid of being labeled in some way." (Interpersonal level, experiential type, medium intensity.)

This last statement allows other group members to comment, without letting Al and Barbara off the hook. It also provides other group members with an opportunity to share their anxieties about the incident. The group leader may wish to introduce, at this point, a structural intervention to facilitate the resolution of the conflict between the two members.

Intervention Outcome

This intervention may allow a freer expression of underlying hostility. Thus, group members could express their feelings about their own reactions to an overt display of hostility. A group norm could then be established, re-examined, and agreed upon. A discussion of aggression and sex roles could also develop, with timely relevance to the group's handling of interpersonal conflict.

Optional Structural Interventions

4. Introspection, p. 211
14. Experiencing Closeness, p. 234

Critical Incident B-27:
Task vs. Maintenance

Theme Topic: Sharpened Affects and Anxieties:
Increased Defensiveness

Context of Incident

In this group, there is a widening split between those group members who support task issues and nonemotional involvements and those who endorse maintenance issues dealing directly with personal feelings. This has sometimes been described as the conflict between "personals" and "structurals," i.e., between those members who wish to explore personal problems and issues ("personals") and those members who generally prefer to avoid personal issues and desire a more formal structure with concrete tasks and goals ("structurals"). In T-groups, this is often called the "task vs. maintenance" issue.

There is a great deal of hostility on the part of each subgroup (task oriented and maintenance oriented) and an inability to see the importance or relevance of the opposing subgroup's position. Following a particularly heated exchange, the group has fallen into a frustrated silence.

Event Preceding Choice Point

The group's silence is broken by two mutually antagonistic statements.

Charlie: "I just can't understand why anyone would want to waste so much time on emotional issues when we need to work on establishing an agenda to get on with our task."

Debbie: "I don't think an agenda has anything to do with what I want from this group. I can't understand your attitude at all."

Various other group members give support to each of these positions and express confusion about opposing stands. The group now lapses into an uneasy silence.

Choice Point

The surface issue is a conflict between two or more group members over the proper group direction, i.e., the pursuit of personal or task issues. The underlying issues are essentially the same and involve decision making at the group level. The leader is faced with a choice-point situation in which he could encourage the group to explore either path, or he could assist the group in understanding and utilizing the resources of both positions. The latter choice is suggested here, although it is recognized that various leaders may prefer a single approach.

What would you do at this point? Give rationale.

Suggested Intervention

First, it is obvious that the leader always has the option of remaining silent, of not responding. This in itself is a type of intervention designed to raise the general anxiety level of the group and sharpen the task-maintenance issue. However, if the leader judges that his continued silence would be unproductive and that the group should first be made aware of the value of integrating and utilizing the two concepts of task and maintenance, then the following intervention can be given.

Group Leader: "I'd like to offer you a few of my observations. For the past thirty minutes, I've been sitting here more and more frustrated with a feeling of being somewhat trapped and with a growing sense of futility. I wonder how many of you feel the same way?" (Group level, experiential type, medium intensity.) This is an experiential sharing by the leader and a reflection of the mood of the group with an invitation to the members to share what they have in common—a sense of frustration.

"Some of the concerns we're expressing here—cognitive vs. emotional—are the same concepts and concerns that man and groups have always struggled with in attempting to create a livable world, the same ones we're struggling with to create our own community, here and now." (Group level, conceptual type, medium intensity.) This response identifies the issues and goals.

The group leader should, by the tone and nature of his intervention, both reflect and discuss the emotional issues involved in this confrontation. The group leader who plays down the emotional issues involved will deliver an intervention of low intensity. Another group leader may prefer to underscore the emotionality of the split in the group and consequently will choose a group-level, high-intensity intervention. He may want to suggest, at this point, a structured experience to help the group deal with its concerns. The structured experience should be concluded with a thorough discussion by all members in order to guide the group to an integrated approach to growth and functioning.

Intervention Outcome

The intent of this intervention is twofold: first, it provides a heightened experiential awareness of the issues involved through the medium of a structured experience; secondly, it provides a supportive climate and technique to guide the resolution of the two opposing issues. If handled successfully, this intervention can be a major step in group growth and cohesion. In turn, it should allow the group to explore the possibilities of utilizing the diverse orientations and resources of all its members in approaching and solving future issues and problems.

Optional Structural Intervention

19. Emotional Self-Sorting, p. 244

Critical Incident B-28: Threatening to Leave

Theme Topic: Sharpened Affects and Anxieties: Increased Defensiveness

Context of Incident

This critical incident occurs during the early to middle stages of group life when the climate and mood of the group invite personal disclosure. In spite of all attempts to establish a nonthreatening and supportive atmosphere, some group members find personal disclosure much too threatening. They express their dislike by threatening to withdraw from the group unless the group changes. This usually occurs because the group has developed no productive means of handling conflict and norms, and some group members attempt to use "membership" as a weapon. This situation may also occur with an individual whose life style demands emotional control almost at all costs. At this point the group has gradually started sharing some personal problems and developing closer emotional ties. However, one or more members may become disturbed over this climate of disclosure.

Event Preceding Choice Point

Eileen (to group leader): "If this type of discussion continues, I don't think I want to attend any more group meetings. I don't want to talk any more about this." Or Eileen may lapse into silence for several sessions, deliberately avoiding this topic, or she may deliberately start missing several meetings.

Choice Point

This critical incident involves one or more issues of reaction to conflict and tension, usually by increased defensiveness and an actual or threatened withdrawal of membership. At the surface level, this is an attempt to manipulate the group into other, safer topics of discussion by threatening to withdraw physically or by continuing to withdraw from membership in the

97

group. At a deeper level, the issue becomes one of membership norms, conflict resolution, and reactions to risk taking and intimacy. If these underlying issues have not been recognized and dealt with appropriately, a member may well consider physical withdrawal as the only realistic alternative. No group member should be forced to risk disclosure in discussing personal topics in the group. However, part of the learning process in growth groups involves working out a satisfactory reciprocal relationship between group expectations and individual needs. If the refusal to discuss issues or even to attend meetings is based on a freely chosen personal decision, there is no substantive problem. If the personal decision is based on fear or an inability to deal with conflict or a lack of trust, however, a deficit in the area of group development is reflected. These issues then should be identified as sources of blockage, as in the instance to be considered here.

What would you do at this point? Give rationale.

Suggested Intervention

Group Leader: "Look, I'd like to stop action for a minute to go over what I consider to be a very crucial point in what just happened. I'd also like to talk for just a minute about conflict and the ways that groups handle it. Typically, when people are experiencing discomfort or anxiety, they may experience other group members exerting pressure—attempting to pour oil on the waters or to persuade or even to coerce them into a different point of view. If all these methods fail, the group may attempt to reject the deviant member. Sometimes these methods will not only be of no use, but they may even drive members further apart. And unless, somehow, a group recognizes and comes to grips with its own typical and particular ways of dealing with conflict, it doesn't learn how to handle a variety of specific situations like the one that has just been occurring in our group." (Group level, conceptual type, medium intensity.) This response series begins with a brief conceptual input on the characteristic ways groups handle conflict.

"What has just happened is very relevant to us all. If you recall, Eileen has fought against this topic . . ." The leader offers a brief recapitulation of the conflict and how the group attempted to handle it, concluded by a description of Eileen's silence, her threat to withdraw, or her absence. "In view of what's been happening here, let's try to be as specific as possible in identifying our feelings about this issue, because apparently Eileen is quite unhappy—and maybe there are others who feel the same way." (Personal/group level, experiential type, medium intensity.)

"The reason I think we should concentrate on this is that, unless we come to grips with this kind of thing, it will continue to happen again and again. And it may get worse each time. So it's not just Eileen's problem. We can't just ignore the phenomenon." (A shift back to group level, conceptual/experiential type, medium intensity.) This intervention removes the pressure from the individual as a deviant member and redirects the issue to the group as a source of legitimate concern and exploration.

Intervention Outcome

This intervention was designed to encourage group members to deal with the issues of the rights and responsibilities of membership, the identification and resolution of conflict, and the establishment of norms regarding silent, absent, or deviant group members. The group may now be able to identify its own characteristic style of responding to such events and, most importantly, evaluate its effect upon all members. This is a major step, by evaluation and productive change, toward increased effectiveness.

Critical Incident B-29: Interrupting Personal Disclosure

Theme Topic: Sharpened Affects and Anxieties: Increased Defensiveness

Context of Incident

About one-third of the group meetings have been held; more and more members are beginning to open up and express deeply personal and intimate topics. As this occurs, some members who have been reticent and reluctant to participate sense that a norm is being established that is both threatening and disturbing. Moreover, they feel uncertain as to their own role and responsibility in the ensuing process. Consequently, the group leader sees pockets of increased defensiveness and sharpened anxieties. In this particular instance, a group member is telling of his own personal history, dealing with his father and mother, bringing in dreams, people, school, etc. Much psychodynamic material is being disclosed to the group.

Event Preceding Choice Point

Fred: "So after that I was pretty confused for a long time, not knowing where to turn, or what direction to take . . ."

After a brief pause, another member intervenes in an abstract but defensive manner that reveals her own underlying anxiety.

Gertrude: "Fred, I feel you're the richer person for having experienced all this. I'm reminded of Maslow's book about how talking about the past is all well and good, but we must begin with where we are now and continue to . . ." This is said with some evidence of nervousness and heightened anxiety that continues for several minutes.

Choice Point

At the surface level, a group member is describing some intensely personal life experiences that, at the time, left him confused and uncertain. At this point, another group member offers help in the form of an abstract piece of advice from a recognized source in the professional literature. Group members may use authoritative advice where it seems appropriate, but they should consider the nature and timing of this advice if it is to be helpful. This was not done here. In addition, the underlying issue in this critical incident deals with a member rushing in with an abstract piece of advice while obviously exhibiting some nervous pressure behind her speech and tension in her body posture. Her intention, apparently because of her personal underlying anxieties, seems to be to remove the focus of concern and attention from a group member prematurely.

What would you do at this point? Give rationale.

Suggested Intervention

There are two general strategies that may be employed in this critical incident. The first approach is to maintain the focus on the individual at the appropriate level of emotion, until he has completed his communication to the group.

Group Leader: "I'm feeling a little uncomfortable at this point, as if Fred had not finished and we cut him off. I'd like to hear more from him as to where he feels all his past has led him and where he is, now, with us." (Individual level, experiential type, low intensity.)

This first intervention ignores Gertrude's motivations and dynamics, since to focus on these underlying issues would draw attention to her and again cut off Fred's sharing of some intensely personal material. However, if Fred has sufficiently completed his interaction with the group, the group leader may wish to intervene and touch upon the underlying issues with Gertrude.

Group Leader: "Gertrude, I'd like to comment on the advice you were giving Fred and try to utilize Maslow's suggestion. I got the feeling that you were empathizing with Fred—as if you were feeling some of his nervousness and anxiety. Sometimes, without being aware of it, we rush in to offer a solution that relieves the pressure that we all feel building up in here. How do you feel about what I've said?" (Individual level, experiential type, medium intensity.)

The purpose of this second intervention is to encourage Gertrude to explore some of her own anxieties and concerns aroused by Fred's disclosures. This is done by using her advice as the basis for discussion and by offering a direction for the discussion to deal with underlying dynamics.

Intervention Outcome

The results of the first intervention will probably bring the group back to a sharing experience with Fred. This should be allowed to continue until he is finished. In the second intervention, Gertrude should be gently encouraged to explore her own underlying feelings. She may simply deny any inner feelings and attempt to defend her advice as emerging from objective, not personal, concerns. Then the group leader will have to decide whether to pursue her defensiveness or to give her more time to open up when she feels less anxious. In either instance the group leader's intervention has recognized possible underlying needs, and this may provide Gertrude with an impetus for thought and change.

Optional Structural Interventions

Critical Incident B-30: Personal vs. Counterpersonal

Theme Topic: Sharpened Affects and Anxieties: Increased Defensiveness

Context of Incident

This critical incident occurs during the early to middle stages of group life and reflects some of the basic issues that may have come up several times before. It is becoming increasingly apparent that group members are pairing or subgrouping around subject-matter issues. In forming these ideological alliances, members find mutual comfort and closeness. This seems to occur over a period of time and is evidenced, for example, by the group's gradually dividing over the "personal versus counterpersonal" orientation. This disagreement as to proper group direction seems to become crystallized in the following dialogue.

Event Preceding Choice Point

Harriet: "Let's forget about personal issues and decide on a concrete project to complete."

Ian: "That sounds like a good idea to me. Maybe we can begin to get something done."

Joyce: "Well, I don't know. It seems to me we *were* getting something done, something important. A project seems sort of incidental to me right now . . ."

Various members agree or disagree strongly.

Choice Point

At the surface level, the problem facing the group is a split between members of two different orientations, centering around the expression of personal feelings and the structuring of experiential activities along some line such as skill development or problem solving. The group is therefore confronted with how to deal with these differences and where to go from here. On a deeper level, members may be reacting to stresses or sharpened anxieties by adopting a defensive position that is more comfortable for them. In so doing the members seek others with whom they share opinions and find a certain amount of safety and protection. If allowed to continue, the differing factions may become more unyielding and consolidated against each other, thus stopping further effective group action.

What would you do at this point? Give rationale.

Suggested Intervention

Group Leader: "We are again facing two apparently different and somewhat antithetical orientations in the group, involving those who are 'personals' and those who are 'counterpersonals.' We have talked about this before, but it is becoming more serious and could conceivably create a breach such that it may become extremely difficult for us to operate in an integrated and collaborative way. So we need to understand what is happening and why it is happening in terms of our own group development. From the very beginning we have had lines that divided us—that is, differences between two or more people that influenced group attitudes.

"As these differences developed, we characteristically observed a pairing phenomenon in which members sought support or a potential ally against ambiguities and uncertainties, as well as perceived personal threats. As time progressed, pairs may have shifted or combined to form larger subgroups. The basis for subgrouping has also shifted to broader issues dealing with interests and special goals. We have certainly run through a number of lines of division! Emerging, then, are issues that are really at the heart of group growth and development. One such issue with which we are now struggling is whether a group can exist as a group with cohesiveness, closeness, productivity, openness, commitment, effective leadership, personal satisfaction, etc., without coming to grips with the question of what kind of emotional or personal 'highway' the group will travel. We begin to see that a lot of the early issues that were dealt with individually and separately have come back again, not in the same way but clustered. The questions are, then, can two apparently different orientations not only reside side by side but also be mutually facilitative? How are we going to bridge the gap between those who judge themselves to be 'personals' and those who judge themselves to be 'counterpersonals'? Understanding the process as I have described it helps, but let me stop and invite you to comment on this issue." (Group level, conceptual type, medium intensity.)

Following this intervention, and with some time for discussion, a second intervention might be indicated to add to the above conceptual framework and provide a means for helping group members come to grips with these issues. This intervention could take the form of a structural intervention.

Intervention Outcome

The structural intervention may introduce more intensive learning and training in effective management of conflict. This intervention is intended to aid in identifying the problem, clarifying the underlying issues, and utilizing specific techniques to help in its resolution. The group may continue to use the principles and observations of group processes gained in this structural intervention as a base for future problem solving. The leader should continue to urge the group to do so, by repeating this pattern whenever necessary.

Optional Structural Intervention

19. Emotional Self-Sorting, p. 244

Critical Incident B-31: Quiet Member

Theme Topic: Sharpened Affects and Anxieties: Increased Defensiveness

Context of Incident

This incident tends to occur in the early to middle stages of group development. The group has generally been discussing such values as trust, intimacy, sharing, and group norms for the disclosure of personal problems. During this discussion, one member of the group has remained quiet and has seemed fearful of joining in group discussions. Finally, one or two of the other group members notice this and comment.

Event Preceding Choice Point

Kurt: "Matt, I notice you haven't said anything or contributed to this group discussion."

Louise: "Yeah, I noticed that, too. Why haven't you said anything?"

Matt (in an emotional tone): "I'll tell you why! I don't feel I can trust the group not to laugh at me or make fun of me if I make a mistake or say something personal and foolish."

This statement appears to have immobilized the other group members and they all focus their attention on this member.

Choice Point

The surface issue involves the refusal of a member to share in the group discussion and risk personal disclosure. At a deeper level, the issue involves trust and mutual concern for other members. If appropriate norms have been established in the group, members should have the freedom to deal with personal issues at almost any level. Therefore, any group process that strengthens a climate of trust and intimacy should be encouraged and reinforced. The leader should respond to the concerns of the individual member as well as attempt to establish the responsibilities of group members for each other. This critical incident is similar to Critical Incident B-33, which deals with a member who has previously experienced a painful self-disclosure. The present critical incident deals, instead, with the anticipatory fears of one or more members.

What would you do at this point? Give rationale.

Suggested Intervention

One alternative would be to say nothing and allow the group to attempt to resolve this issue. This might lead members to express themselves personally on such issues as trust, dependency, risk taking, involvement, and intimacy. However, if silence does not lead the members to initiate productive discussion, another intervention might focus on the reasons for the group's sudden silence. A third, more direct intervention follows.

Group Leader: "I'm really glad to hear you say what you did, Matt, because to me it's a very honest statement and one that I respect. I feel that it represents a risk for you to have said this aloud to the others. In a way it's paradoxical, because in your statement to the group, you have assumed a greater risk than in remaining silent and not disclosing yourself." (Individual level, experiential type, medium intensity, with an immediate move to a conceptual type to give the individual supportive feedback.) "I wonder how the rest of us feel in dealing with the trust issue and disclosure?" (A shift to group level, conceptual type, low intensity.)

After the group has devoted some time to the sharing of ideas and feelings and the intensity has dropped, it is relevant to introduce a brief recap of what just occurred.

Group Leader: "Let's take a moment to look at what has just happened. I think it's a beautiful example of how we can be supportive and help build bridges of trust by our willingness to reveal our concerns and to acknowledge that we all have, at times, shared these concerns. I don't know how you feel, but I feel just a little bit more comfortable about sharing, and I wonder if the rest of you do," (Individual level, experiential type, low intensity, to facilitate climate setting and the opportunity for future sharing at a deeper, more comfortable level.) Following this intervention, the leader has the option of introducing a structural intervention involving giving and accepting trust.

Intervention Outcome

This intervention was presented at several levels to allow the leader selectively to emphasize those issues and concerns considered most important. All the interventions, however, are designed to (1) respect the concerns of the individual; (2) show, by asking for feedback, that certain concerns are common among the rest of the group; (3) tie these concerns to important group issues such as trust, intimacy, and risk taking; and (4) suggest a structural intervention that is designed to emphasize these concerns and at the same time to encourage their resolution. The discovery of mutually shared concerns involving disclosure will aid all members in assuming responsibility for membership in future critical incidents involving trust.

Optional Structural Interventions

5. Surrender and Support, p. 213
20. The Hand Press, p. 245

Critical Incident B-32: Red-Crossing

Theme Topic: Sharpened Affects and Anxieties: Increased Defensiveness

Context of Incident

This critical incident, occurring during the early to middle part of group life, is usually observed immediately following an emotional, painful disclosure of some intensity by a group member. Typically other members rush in with supportive, comforting statements, which reduce the tension and block the individual from any further painful disclosure ("red-crossing"). As a result of this emotional sharing, the climate of the group may be described as an anxious closeness. Several, if not all, group members are involved.

Event Preceding Choice Point

The group response to this critical incident may occur in a nonverbal way, as when a group member gets up and goes over to sit beside or put his arm around the individual. It may also take a verbal form.

Noel: "I really appreciate your courage in telling us that, Ron."

Ord: "I really have a great deal of respect and love for you, now."

Penny: "I guess we've all had things that bothered us, in the group, and I appreciate your sharing your feelings with us."

Choice Point

The surface issue involves giving support and encouragement to a member who has started relating painful personal events. It is important to note that premature support of a member in this situation may alleviate the group's anxiety but at the same time block further exploration by the individual. This may be seen as "red-crossing" or "band-aiding" of the individual and is an expected response on the part of some group members. The underlying issues that prompt this group behavior are usually reactions to the sharpened anxieties and defensiveness present as well as problems of intimacy and control. If this "repair work" follows a finished process, it is productive and adds to the cohesion of all members. However, premature support encourages the individual to terminate his personal exploration and essentially blocks further growth. The group leader needs to decide which of the two situations exists.

What would you do at this point? Give rationale.

Suggested Intervention

Group Leader: "Let me share an image and a feeling with you. I get the image of trying to tie a bow on a package and whatever is inside is nice and neatly packaged. We've tied the bow and placed it over here, in a corner. Maybe what I'm saying is that Ron has been nicely packaged, or at least his feelings have, and I feel uncomfortable because they were wrapped up so quickly." (Group level, experiential/conceptual type, medium intensity.)

"A number of members have said some very supportive things concerning Ron's expression of feelings. I'm not questioning that these were meant well with kindness and sincerity and concern, but their impact is to wrap up Ron with all those streams of expression. I think we should look at this, because even with the best intentions, we can block other things from happening that might be even more useful, though painful. Sometimes when people say things like 'I appreciate what you've done in here,' they're in effect saying, 'You're finished with what you've been saying,' and it has the effect of slowing or even stopping things and preventing any further work. Part of the difficulty, I think, is in 'red-crossing' or 'band-aiding' or repairing 'holes in emotional dikes.' Although it's more uncomfortable, I think it's sometimes necessary to help someone experience things more painfully, rather than just providing aid and comfort." (Group level, conceptual type, medium intensity.) This response points out issues involved in the past process.

"I believe, Ron, that you said a great many painful things, but I have the feeling you were not finished." (A shift to individual level, experiential type, low intensity.) The focus here is on the feelings previously cut off.

"Perhaps an alternative to what we did would be, at the very least, an attempt to help you to get at some of the things behind your statements. What I'm saying is that we need to be aware of what we're doing. Ron, let me ask you: Do you feel finished? Do you feel like going on?" (Individual level, experiential type, low intensity.)

Intervention Outcome

The interventions offer Ron the option of continuing with his personal exploration or stopping the process at that point. Often an individual will state that he does not wish to continue at the present time but will do so later. Equally often, an individual will slowly continue to present his concerns to the group. The group should then be encouraged to support the individual, offer its resources as help, and allow the process to be finished before it is "packaged." This allows the group to develop more appropriate techniques for the reduction of anxiety and the resolution of problems.

Optional Structural Interventions

15. Saying Good-Bye, p. 235
18. Peeling Emotional Layers, p. 242

Critical Incident B-33: A Member Cries

Theme Topic: Sharpened Affects and Anxieties: Increased Defensiveness

Context of Incident

This critical incident occurs during the early to middle stages of group life. The climate of the group has been steadily moving toward more and more intimacy. The group has just finished a general discussion on trust. In the brief silence that ensues, a group member who has remained silent throughout most of the conversation suddenly begins to cry.

Event Preceding Choice Point

Sam (crying): "I wouldn't want anyone to open up inside, not anyone! It's horrible and it can make you miserable. I've tried it and I know! It's too big a risk to take!" Sam continues crying.

The other group members appear shocked and taken aback by this incident, silently looking at Sam or the group leader.

Choice Point

The surface issue involves deciding whether to inquire about the reasons for Sam's discomfort, to comfort him or respectfully ignore his distress, or to offer any comment to the entire group. The underlying issues center around concerns of intimacy, inclusion, increased anxiety, and risk taking.

The group leader may choose to emphasize any or all of these issues, but it is suggested that the problem of trust may be a major concern of all members. The issue of trust centers about the following questions: "How much can I trust myself—and others?" "How far can I go in revealing personal data?" "How far do I want other members to go?" "What are the responsibilities of members to those who choose to reveal personal information?" The group leader is facing a situation in which personal disclosure has resulted in overt distress on the part of a member. In order to prevent this situation from inhibiting other group members, care must be exercised in handling Sam's intense emotion.

What would you do at this point? Give rationale.

Suggested Intervention

Initially the most preferable option would be simply to remain sympathetically silent, waiting to see if the group could successfully handle Sam's distress. If the group appears unable or unwilling to do so, the group leader might offer the following comments.

Group Leader: "Sam, I appreciate how you must feel right now, and I respect your statement about not being willing to risk disclosing your insides. Yet, now I see more of you disclosed in your attempt not to do so than I ever would have if you had remained silent. In many ways, you risked more by saying what you did—and you're risking more at this moment for us than you probably realize. Let me say that I respect and care for you and feel closer to you than ever before. I don't know how the others feel, but you've had an impact on me." (Individual level, experiential type, low intensity.)

This statement should be followed by silence on the part of the leader to give the group a chance to respond. If the group does respond appropriately, a feeling of group unity and cohesion will be facilitated and will enable future sharing on a deeper, more intimate level. However, if the group attempts to ignore Sam, or starts off on another discussion topic to avoid dealing with an emotional issue, the leader might adopt an intervention approach in which he reviews events and encourages members to respond overtly to the current dilemma.

Intervention Outcome

If the leader's silence results in other members generally supporting the distressed member, the emotional cohesion among members will have been strengthened. Occasionally a member may rise from his seat and put his arm around the upset member's shoulders or hold his hand, during which very little is said. These are behaviors that indicate group growth through shared concern and support.

The leader may briefly indicate his pleasure at the manner in which the situation was handled. This second intervention would model behavior for other members. In addition to a verbal intervention of support, the leader may wish to present a structural intervention dealing directly with the issue of trust. In this approach, the group member is allowed directly to experience emotional risk taking and trust, followed by a discussion of the implications for the group.

Optional Structural Interventions

5. Surrender and Support, p. 213

16. Affection Blanket, p. 237

17. Group and Individual Journeys into Fantasy, p. 239

Critical Incident B-34: Token Disclosure

Theme Topic: *Sharpened Affects and Anxieties: Increased Defensiveness*

Context of Incident

This critical incident usually occurs during the beginning to early/middle phases of group life. If the group members are especially intellectual, formal, and nonexpressive, it may not emerge until the middle stage.

The group as a whole has now made a few tentative thrusts at dealing with emotional issues. Two or three group members have revealed some personal concerns to the group, accompanied by displays of appropriate emotion. Following these emotional disclosures, the group climate seems to be one of quietness and tranquility, with group members continuing to rework and reaffirm the importance of the personal disclosures. An inertia has developed, leading to a group collusion to avoid future painful issues. It is becoming obvious that the group considers this to be a final, token gesture to the emotional aspects of group work.

Event Preceding Choice Point

Terry: "I really feel close to John after our talk: I think I know, now, how he *really* feels."

Vicki: "I think we're all closer now than we've ever been. It seems we really trust each other."

Walt: "I feel the same way. This group seems very solid and completely supportive."

Yvonne: "You know what we ought to do? We should all get together and go somewhere and drink beer and have ourselves a little party."

Other members continue the conversation along the same lines.

Choice Point

The group leader must exercise judgment at this point as to whether this type of mutual support and approval should be encouraged and reinforced as a reflection of appropriate behavior on the part of the group. If it is a sincere attempt to provide mutual support, it should be encouraged to facilitate personal growth. However, when groups begin talking about how warm, close, and open they are, they can block or avoid unresolved issues. This is a "flight into health" and a reaction to the increasing conflict and tension emerging in the group. It may be seen as an attempt to establish a norm of "maintaining the happy status quo."

What would you do at this point? Give rationale.

Suggested Intervention

It is preferable to direct interventions at the group level initially, in an effort to preserve the healthy aspects of personal sharing and exposure while pointing out the underlying avoidance behavior of the group.

Group Leader: "You know, I think some of the things that have been going on during this session are very important. I want to share my feelings about it, not from the point of view of trying to burst our bubble or minimizing the intense feelings involved. I'd like you to think of my comments as making it possible to move on and not be fixed at some level of inability to experience more pain." (Group level, conceptual type, low intensity.) This intervention is an analysis of the experience in terms of future growth.

"Sometimes groups become fixed, or frozen, after going through a common emotional experience. It's as if they develop a positive evaluation of it which tends to lock in the process—people don't want to open things up to any other left-over negative feelings. This sense of well-being, which is justified in part, may get in the way of future explorations. And what you find a group doing is 'circling,' that is, going around and around, restating historically the work it has done, looking to its history rather than to its future. It's like saying, 'Our wound has been opened and bled, and we're doing very well. We're healing. We don't want to open up any more wounds.' The remarks made by Terry, and you, Walt, reflect both sides of this issue." (A movement from group to interpersonal level, conceptual type, medium intensity.)

"The more we are locked into this mold, the harder it is for each of us to be honest in confronting another person with those sources of conflict or friction, especially with negative remarks. Do you see what I'm saying? How do you feel about what I've just said?" (A shift back to group level; a movement from conceptual to experiential type, from medium to low intensity.) This intervention invites the participation of all members.

Intervention Outcome

The group leader has attempted (1) to analyze both surface and underlying issues in terms of both positive and negative aspects of the process; (2) to selectively reinforce and preserve those issues dealing with personal growth through disclosure and group sharing, while at the same time subtly discouraging a premature closure of emotional expression; and (3) to encourage the possibility of continued growth in a specific direction.

Occasionally, a group member may reply to this intervention in the following manner.

Group Member: "It seems like you're always wanting everybody to suffer all the time, and people have enough problems as it is, without being oversensitive to unpleasant things. It's hard enough just to go on living, without letting little things bug you all the time. You're always expecting me to hate people, and to be angry at them, and I just don't feel that much."

Group Leader: "Is that what you heard me say? Did anyone else hear that? Would someone care to restate what I just said?" (Individual level, experiential type, low intensity; then a shift to group level.) This response prevents the group leader from becoming a "professional summarizer" and places more responsibility on the group to provide corrective feedback.

Optional Structural Interventions

17. Group and Individual Journeys into Fantasy, p. 239
18. Peeling Emotional Layers, p. 242

MIDDLE CRITICAL INCIDENTS

Critical Incident M-1: Twenty Questions

Theme Topic: Sharpened Interactions: Growth-Identifying Activities and Reality Strengthening

Context of Incident

During the middle stages of group life, the general mood or climate of the group has progressed to the point where members become "explorers" of each other's personality. Whereas earlier group behavior toward a member may have been marked by hostility or superficial concern, these middle stages usually reveal a probing, but nonhelpful, style best described as "twenty questions." There are no specific personality styles or characteristics involved, since all group members are prone to join in the questioning. This in-depth questioning blocks close attention to other group issues.

Event Preceding Choice Point

Aaron (following a brief discussion of a personal problem of concern): "So, that's what made me so depressed at that time."
Betty: "Then what did you do?"
Carole: "Did you ever consider divorce?"
Dick: "What about the effect on your job?"
The group continues along this line and style of inquiry.

Choice Point

While individual group members may, from time to time, exhibit this questioning pattern of behavior, it has become a standard approach for the majority of members during this period of group life. This behavior tends to be more destructive than helpful to an individual. The issues tend to be clustered about such concerns as group style, exposure, risk taking, and the helping relationship. Although the surface behavior appears to be one of concerned inquiry, closer inspection usually reveals little or no utilization of the data in helpful feedback. The group leader must judge if the group style is developing along these lines, evaluate the extent of helpfulness, and then intervene in such a manner as to increase the effectiveness of the helping relationship while at the same time preserving the supportive orientation of the group. The leader's attempt is to sharpen up the interactions and point out growth-identifying activities.

What would you do at this point? Give rationale.

Suggested Intervention

Group Leader: "I wonder if we might stop for a moment and look at what's been happening? From time to time, as groups grow and develop together, certain fairly consistent patterns tend to emerge as members begin learning how to work together. We've already identified a couple of these—remember the 'sharpshooter' and 'battleship' style we talked about earlier? It seems that we are now evolving a style that might best be identified as 'twenty questions.' That is, someone discusses a problem or a feeling, and everyone begins to dissect it, piece by piece, by asking questions and probing. And this can be okay, but if that's all there is, I wonder if something isn't missing?" (Group level, conceptual type, medium intensity.) This intervention briefly describes the evolutionary pattern of growth in the group as a series of emerging group styles.

"I wonder, Aaron, if I might ask you whether you felt very helped by these twenty questions?" (A shift to individual level, experiential type, low intensity.) This places the immediate behavior into the theoretical framework and asks for evaluation. The group member will usually answer that he has not felt particularly helped by this probing and questioning. On those infrequent occasions when the group member automatically and defensively states that he was helped, the leader should ask, "In what specific ways were you helped?" The group member is usually able to give little or no data to support his statement.

"How do the rest of you feel about what's just been happening in the group?" (Group level, experiential type, low intensity.) This statement provides the opportunity for the group to respond to the process just identified.

The group leader may want to suggest an activity helpful in identifying a problem issue, clarifying it, looking at some possible means of resolution, and utilizing the group's resources in the service of an individual.

Intervention Outcome

This intervention has the following goals: (a) identification of the issues involved in the ongoing group process, (b) group discussion of the problem with attention toward group style, and (c) a suggested structural intervention to provide a more effective means of identifying and resolving important concerns within a helping relationship framework. Ranging from conceptual to experiential to structural, this entire intervention recapitulates the proper "modeling" for the group, i.e., identifying the problem, clarifying the issues involved, and using specific resources to aid in its resolution.

Optional Structural Intervention

21. The O-P-Q-R Exercise, p. 247

Critical Incident M-2: Psychoanalyst

Theme Topic: Sharpened Interactions: Growth-Identifying Activities and Reality Strengthening

Context of Incident

This incident occurs during the middle stages of the group, when the climate has become sufficiently supportive to allow some probing among group members. The "psychoanalyst" pattern is a more subtle and sophisticated version of "twenty questions," the essential difference being that "twenty questions" typically begins and ends with a series of questions, while "psycho-analyst" typically picks up at this point and offers an explanatory concept that has the effect of closing off further discussion. This style may be loaded with psychological jargon. It presents an intellectual but superficial inter-pretation of a member's motivations and behavior. This group style may also represent an attempt to establish and crystallize certain group norms of "helpfulness." It should be noted that "psychoanalyst" may also be an individual life style developed by some group members as an intellectual defense and may have been in evidence since the early group stages. At this point, this behavior begins seriously to interfere with both individual and group functioning.

Event Preceding Choice Point

Edie (following an intense account of her difficulties with men, particularly men in this group): "And so, I've always feared saying or doing anything such that they would put me down."

Frank: "From what you've told us, it sounds like it all started with your father. You had an unfortunate early life, and now you probably hate all men as a result of this experience—probably hate older men most of all. That's understandable."

George: "How do you feel about older men? Hostile? Ambivalent?"

Choice Point

This critical incident requires that an individual style be identified as it inter-acts with other group members. Often, this "psychoanalyst" approach will be adopted by several group members. As with Critical Incident M-1, the recurrent issues are those of group style, exposure, risk taking, and the helping relationship. Although an ostensible attempt is made to help the individual by growth-identifying activities, the approach tends to focus on the "diseases" of the organism that have expressed themselves so far. This critical incident revolves around group style, with individual style as a secondary concern.

What would you do at this point? Give rationale.

Suggested Intervention

Group Leader: "I wonder if we could stop action for a moment to ask what's been going on for the last several minutes?" (Group level, experiential type, low intensity.)

This intervention invites feedback from the group on their observations. Usually, group members will simply state that a certain member was relating a problem to which a solution was given.

"Edie, you've certainly been given a number of reasons or explanations as to the causes of your difficulties: I wonder—have they been helpful?" (A pause for a reply or nod.) "Regardless of their degree of correctness, I certainly sense clinical attempts to interpret feelings and motivation at the unconscious level. Could someone else check me out on this?" (A pause for response.) "How do the rest of you feel?" (A pause.) "It seems that we might be experiencing a more sophisticated version of 'twenty questions': it's called 'psychoanalyst.' I guess we all have a tendency to analyze and offer solutions, but maybe there's a more helpful way of tackling the problems we have. I would like to suggest an activity that's been very useful for identifying a problem, clarifying it, and looking at some possible alternatives for resolution. It's a way of really 'zeroing in' on our resources in the service of an individual. It's called The O-P-Q-R Exercise." (Group level, structural type, medium intensity.) The purpose of this exercise is to introduce more intensive learning and training in effective interpersonal problem solving. (See Critical Incident M-1.)

Intervention Outcome

It is anticipated that the group will continue to utilize the principles and observations of group process gained in the structural activity as a base for future problem solving.

Optional Structural Interventions

1. Empathic Communication, p. 205
21. The O-P-Q-R Exercise, p. 247

Critical Incident M-3: How Are We Doing?

Theme Topics: Sharpened Interactions: Growth-Identifying
Activities and Reality Strengthening
Decreased Defensiveness and Increased
Experimentation

Context of Incident

This critical incident takes place in the middle to end phases of group life. It is concerned with the manner in which a group becomes interested in an evaluation of its progress and maturity. The group is at least partially aware of its growth, but members seek independent evaluation. It is concerned with leadership, authority relations, and group goals. This group, after a number of false starts in various directions, has apparently chosen a productive pathway. During the discussion that follows, a group member may request an evaluation.

Event Preceding Choice Point

Gloria: "In your experience as a group leader, what are the signs that a group is moving in the proper direction?"

Choice Point

On the surface, this is a direct request for information. The underlying issues that lead to this situation are varied and intertwined. This situation could be approached from the issue of authority or of leadership; e.g., "Are you dissatisfied with the group's behavior? Are we doing O.K.?" Points that must be considered: In what direction is the group moving? Is it a proper direction? Is it moving at all? These issues should be recognized in any intervention by the leader.

What would you do at this point? Give rationale.

Suggested Intervention

Group Leader: "Gloria, let me respond to your question as I have to several other people, by trying to identify the two levels at which you are communicating. Your statement was, on the surface, a request for information regarding guidelines and yardsticks with which to evaluate our growth and development; and I think that is a legitimate and highly relevant question at this time. But, on the second level, I hear you asking something like 'Tell us how we are doing. Are we a good group?' Sometimes, with similar questions, I have seen this as an attempt to control my behavior. I don't view this as that kind of control now, but it is a subtle way to reinstate me in a kind of paternal position, so that I might possibly 'pat you on the back.'" (Individual level, conceptual type, medium intensity.) To return the matter to the group, the leader shifts levels:

"I think we are moving, and moving well. On the other hand, the question at hand is 'Where do we turn to find out how we're doing?' On what criteria do we rely and who are the sources for such criteria? Certainly you can go to papers on group growth and on issues of trust, openness, testing, etc. You can rely on the authority of the printed word, but you already have that. So this leads me to believe that this isn't primarily a request for information but a request to get me to give you—the group—a fatherly hug and tell you how good you have been. What do you, Gloria, and the others feel?" (Group level, conceptual type, medium intensity.)

Intervention Outcome

This intervention may motivate the group to discuss these issues, their feelings about the group's growth, and their own sense of direction as well as their views on the leader's role. Frequently the person involved will deny the underlying dependency and get support from the group. This allows discussion of authority issues and personal experiences that gave rise to individual attitudes. Notice that the legitimate request for information was quickly answered. This incident again points out the possibility of mixed motivations in any given request and also illustrates how groups may reach the point of reducing their defenses and of engaging in increased experimentation as to new ways to reach goals.

Critical Incident M-4: Are We Finished?

Theme Topic: Sharpened Interactions: Growth-Identifying Activities and Reality Strengthening

Context of Incident

This critical incident occurs when the members feel they can handle issues in a variety of ways and want to finish an issue that has a few loose threads but has almost been completed. They question their ability to recognize underlying issues. This incident involves group style and group norms. Here the group has just finished talking about why a group member did not take a risk and what they could have done to help her and help the group. The group at this point is engaging in sharpened interactions based on reality-strengthening and growth-identifying activities.

Event Preceding Choice Point

Hank: "I guess we can move on."

    Inez: "Yeah, but I feel like she's still on a hot seat, kind of . . ."

    Jack: "I feel that, too. But I don't know what else to do. I feel like we're on a dime."

    Kathy: "I feel like she's on a dime."

    Louise: "I feel that we all are, and we can't move from here!"

Choice Point

The surface issue and the real issue appear to be the same. When has an issue been worked? How can the group move on without minimizing or avoiding the issues it leaves behind? This involves group style, decision making, and the resolution of conflict (to move on or to stay here). One alternative for the leader is to have the group consider the conceptual aspects of when change is appropriate, as well as how to move. Another alternative is to help the group decide how to "break" a group mood and the influence of the mood on subsequent behavior. A third alternative is to change the mood or at least interrupt it momentarily.

What would you do at this point? Give rationale.

Suggested Intervention

An example of the third alternative follows:

Group Leader: "I'd like to suggest something. At this point if we could just take a couple of minutes and stand up and turn around. Think for a minute of what we could do when we come back that would get us off the dime. Otherwise, we're going to just sit here and be stuck. Would you be willing to do that? Think about what you might personally do when we turn around that would really move us. How would you personally get involved to break the set?" (Group level, structural type, low intensity.)

Intervention Outcome

This intervention used a low-intensity structural intervention to break the climate or mood of a group, as well as the physical set. Often group members need only a slight shift in behavior to get them moving in a productive direction. This simple structural intervention allows members to try out different methods of response once they turn around and sit down again in the group. Sometimes a simple act of taking a five-minute break will serve sufficiently to alter the atmosphere of the group.

Optional Structural Intervention

22. Behavior Prescription, p. 249

Critical Incident M-5: Past History

Theme Topic: Sharpened Interactions: Growth-Identifying Activities and Reality Strengthening

Context of Incident

At this midpoint in group life, many members have gained insight into their own interpersonal difficulties and are attempting to work productively. One group member with a number of serious personality problems insists on bringing up past events. Although he does not seem to have profited by the group's help in the past, he is now threatening to sway the group by airing problems he has brought up many times before.

Event Preceding Choice Point

Matt: "I can tell you from personal experience how hard it is to make a decision. There were times, during my first two years at work, that my boss always seemed to disagree or be rubbed wrong by something I said. He seemed irritated and . . ."

Choice Point

In situations such as that described above, the clinical judgment of the leader becomes quite important in determining whether this is a legitimate issue for the group to wrestle with or whether it would be more productive for the group to continue with the business at hand. There are times when a group may be vulnerable and easily seduced into dealing with problems that are nonproductive for both the individual and the group. Another related issue is the extent to which a group may legitimately be able to help individuals with deep-seated problems of a pervasive nature. The valid evaluation by a group of its ability to handle just such issues represents growth-identifying activities and provides a stronger sense of reality testing.

What would you do at this point? Give rationale.

Suggested Intervention

There are several options for the group leader, arranged in order of preference. The first intervention would be to remain silent and to allow the group to handle whatever was happening. If no one intervenes and the group begins to falter, the next-preferred intervention would be to encourage someone in the group to try to summarize or conceptualize the process now going on.

Group Leader: "I wonder if anyone would like to try and describe what has gone on in the past few minutes?" (Group level, conceptual type, low intensity.)

This second intervention is usually sufficient to draw the appropriate responses from the group members. If, however, the group continues to be immobilized, the leader may say:

"Matt, I want you to know that I hear you, but in the interest of our being able to complete our decision making, I would prefer that you hold off on that for a while, if possible, since I feel we're on the verge of making some decisions vital to the group." (Individual level, experiential type, medium intensity.) This intervention does not deny the importance of the individual's statement but attempts to place it in its proper perspective within the group.

If, in spite of these interventions, Matt persists in tying up the group with a recurrent theme or problem, one which the group is unable to handle, the following intervention may be in order.

Group Leader: "Matt, let me give you this observation: I've noticed a number of times this same problem has arisen from you, attempting to influence us to think in certain terms with you—or for you—in order to help you, but it gets us off the track and blocks us from doing other kinds of things. I know you want to get on with other kinds of learning, too, and I want to draw to your attention the fact that the group has been persistently prevented from doing this." (Individual level, experiential type, medium intensity.) This response attempts to delimit the problem as primarily an individual concern, rather than a legitimate group activity.

Intervention Outcome

This intervention sequence was designed to allow the group to handle the problem if at all possible. Following this alternative, a gradual "fading-in" of leader interventions is employed, beginning with simple interventions that point out the important cues and leading to more pointed interventions that dramatize the process. This orientation assumes that the group is now at a point where the members are able to take responsibility for their own behavior. It is based on a theory of distributive leadership wherein members are encouraged to provide more and more of their own leadership interventions before the group leader assumes specialized responsibility; that is, the group leader with a distributive-leadership orientation waits to see if some member of the group will intervene effectively.

Critical Incident M-6: Asking Permission

Theme Topics: Sharpened Interactions: Growth-Identifying
Activities and Reality Strengthening
Decreased Defenses and
Increased Experimentation

Context of Incident

This critical incident occurs in the middle to end phases of group life when members begin to assume more leadership functions, take on more responsibility for group growth, and be more willing to take risks and experiment with new behaviors. This behavior is a mark of the maturity of the group and the involvement of members in their own growth, knowledge, and skills.

Event Preceding Choice Point

Nancy, who has been highly verbal, insensitive to others, and authoritarian, has lapsed into silence for a few sessions. She then makes the following statement.

"I'd like to ask the group if anyone would mind if I tried something. I'd like to try it, but if anyone objects I'll just let it go."

Choice Point

The surface issue is whether or not the group should go along with the request of one of its members. The underlying issues are the responsibilities of the members to each other and the handling of new behaviors in the service of group growth. It also shows a change in Nancy's perception of authority roles and her attitude toward being in such roles. It may provide an opportunity for personal growth.

What would you do at this point? Give rationale.

Suggested Intervention

Group Leader: "I was really happy to see that, because, until today, it seems to me you haven't sought the opinions of others before proceeding toward your goals." (Individual level, experiential type, low intensity.) "But you now seem really concerned. Apparently, you are no longer determined to force your opinions. And I for one am glad to see it." (Individual level, experiential type, medium intensity.)

Intervention Outcome

Nancy may use this reinforcement to continue her personal growth. The intervention went from low to medium intensity to heighten the effect. The comments may encourage other group members as well to try out new behaviors by demonstrating that the risk may not be as high as they thought. The group may take this into consideration when deciding whether to grant Nancy's request. This involves growth for Nancy as well as for the group. Often, the responsibility of the members to the group is discussed more than the group's responsibility to individual members, and this critical incident could help bridge that gap. It also illustrates a degree of decreased defensiveness on the part of the member who wishes to try out the new behavior.

Critical Incident M-7: Meanwhile, Back in the Real World . . .

Theme Topic: Norm Crystallization/Enforcement-Defensification

Context of Incident

At some point during the middle stages of the group, when members become anxious over the establishment of workable norms, there may be an attempt to turn the group into a discussion seminar focusing on one or more "real world" issues such as politics or religion. Several anxious group members have avoided dealing with any interpersonal issues for the last few sessions. In this session a few members have launched into a discussion over the forthcoming imposition of rules on their outside social organization by their administrative hierarchy. Some are for it, some are against it, some are indifferent. Several minutes have passed, with the members debating the merits of both positions.

Event Preceding Choice Point

Owen: "And that's how I feel about the whole question of how it's structured."

There is a short pause. It is obvious that the conversational trend will continue.

Choice Point

The question for the group leader is whether to allow the political discussion to continue or to bring the group's attention back to here-and-now concerns. It should be recognized that these are not mutually exclusive concerns. Indeed, a discussion of the need for the imposition of rules may reflect underlying concerns about the apparent lack of norms in the group. If this latter situation appears to be the case, the group leader should point this

139

out as a specific example of underlying concerns being expressed in surface topics. However, the group may simply be "hooked" on an emotionally charged outside topic that is irrelevant to the goals of the group. The group leader must decide between these two alternatives and intervene accordingly.

What would you do at this point? Give rationale.

Suggested Intervention

When a group is hooked on an interesting topic that is irrelevant to the needs of the group, the leader may say:

"I've noticed that for quite some time now we've been talking about an issue that has arisen outside the group. It seems it gives some of us a direction and topic—but I wonder what it has to do with us as a group, our getting to know each other?" (Group level, conceptual type, low intensity.) This statement may be all that is needed to get the group to examine carefully its present behavior and motivations.

If the group leader senses that the discussion centering about structure is really reflecting underlying concerns over the absence of group norms, another intervention would be called for.

Group Leader: "You know, we seem to be quite concerned in our discussion today over the question of structure, rules, and the enforcement of norms and whether these are needed or not. It occurs to me that we may be talking about more than just an abstract idea: I wonder if we're perhaps expressing some of our own concerns, in here, over lack of rules, norms, and direction? Does anyone else feel this way or have some thoughts about this?" (Group level, conceptual type, medium intensity.)

Intervention Outcome

The results of the first intervention may serve to stimulate group discussion about the motivation and need to discuss an outside topic. If the irrelevant discussion persists, the group leader might wish to intervene in order to obtain feedback on his own perceptions.

The second intervention was designed to sensitize group members to the possible and frequent connection between surface behavior and underlying concerns. The subsequent discussion of underlying concerns and anxieties should provide one more step toward interpersonal cohesiveness and the establishment of group norms that are enforceable and realistic.

Optional Structural Intervention

7. Group Observing Group, p. 217

Critical Incident M-8: Rites of Passage

Theme Topic: Norm Crystallization/Enforcement-Defensification

Context of Incident

Often found in the middle stages of group life, this incident involves membership norms and group style and is an attempt by some members to coerce other group members into performing the so-called "rites of passage." In this incident, the group leader observes a series of events in which one group member after another is expected to go through a pattern of behavior such as "confession"—an intimate self-disclosure or crying—and then be welcomed into the group as a full-fledged "member."

Event Preceding Choice Point

Pete: "Okay, Ron, how about telling us something about yourself?"
    Sarah: "Yeah, you're divorced, aren't you?"
    Ron proceeds to relate personal, sometimes painful material. When he finishes, a woman with anxiety in her voice starts talking about a related intimate incident. This procedure continues on around the group, with some members encouraging others to confess.

Choice Point

The surface issue involves what behaviors the members of the group will express or resist according to the norms of the group. The underlying issues involve intimacy, the acceptance of rules without discussion or consensus, and the control of the group by tacit collusion to allow some members collectively to dictate to the majority of members.

What would you do at this point? Give rationale.

Suggested Intervention

Group Leader: "I'd like to take a minute and talk about something that's been going on and try to give you a "handle" that may be useful. For a couple of sessions now, certain group members have tried to set a direction for the whole group that has to do with what we might call the 'rites of passage.' What I mean is that there has been a mounting pressure that members must overtly express themselves to the group in order for them to qualify for group membership and/or the next level of shared involvement. Somehow, there seems to be a growing pressure that each of us has to go through some type of emotional upheaval, or some personal testimony or pain, or some highly intense expression of feeling that builds up to a crisis-like proportion that is then worked through. And this really has been happening, wouldn't you say?" (Group level, conceptual type, high intensity.)

This intervention has brought the group's attention to what some members have been doing in order to regulate behaviors. This brief feedback to the group is to prepare them to respond after the next brief theory input.

"On the other hand, as pressure has been mounting for this type of behavior, I think there has been a corresponding or associated increase in resistance. So I guess some of us, those who have had this type of experience, have pushed while others have resisted, and maybe some of us have been both pushing and resisting, thereby revealing our ambivalent feelings toward this kind of deep personal expression.

"A term I use to describe this phenomenon is 'pluralistic ignorance.' It says, in effect, that until a norm or standard is tested, it may very well be that practically everybody in the group thinks that other people in the group want a certain kind of behavior or want affairs to be conducted in a certain way, and each person thinks that he is the only one who objects—so he will 'go along.' And if everyone in the group feels this way, most or even all of the members of a group might be conforming to a norm that *no* individual wants. That's pluralistic ignorance." (Group level, conceptual type, medium intensity.)

"I believe that we want to moderate if not reject outright the sharp edge, the hurting edge, of 'rites of passage,' but we don't want to make it impossible for people to express themselves and we don't want to indicate in any way that it isn't good to cry if you feel like crying or that we shouldn't put pressure on people who deceive or dissemble, especially in regard to their own feelings. But it does mean that we may be doing ourselves a disservice, preventing group and individual growth, if we try to legislate a rite of passage, because a true emotional movement can only evolve spontaneously and when there is no sense of constraint." (Group level, conceptual type, medium intensity.)

Intervention Outcome

This intervention may maintain the commitment and serious mood that had been established under the guise of group pressure but change the focus from "what members should do" to "how members feel about certain controls they are accepting." This may also provide the basis for concrete evaluation of certain implicit, untested standards that group members have been following.

Critical Incident M-9: Urging Participation

Theme Topic: Norm Crystallization/Enforcement-Defensification

Context of Incident

During the middle stages of group life, one or more group members may be silent or reluctant to participate, perhaps even refusing to do so. This may be a temporary reaction to tension, or it may represent a taciturn individual life style. Other members may often urge these individuals to participate. This may occur after other topics have been exhausted by more active members, who then search for another focus. In order to reduce the ensuing anxiety over periods of silence, less verbal members are urged to participate.

Event Preceding Choice Point

Tom: "John, why haven't you shared anything of yourself with us?"
    Vicki: "John hasn't said *anything*. I'd like to hear from John!"
    John: "I guess I really don't have much to say."
    At this point, some members may be persistent.
    Walt: "Well, I'd still like to hear from you! Don't you have anything to say?"
    Other members may then become supportive.
    Zach: "Well, that's all right. If he doesn't feel like saying anything, then that's his business."
    Other members become similarly involved.

Choice Point

The surface issue is whether a group member should respond or be allowed to remain silent. The underlying issue involves the development of norms and standards regarding the acceptability of differences in individual members' styles and the rights of the group versus the rights of the individual. It is important to intervene in a manner that will facilitate recognition of these underlying issues.

What would you do at this point? Give rationale.

Suggested Intervention

Group Leader: "What just took place is pretty significant to us in terms of the whole question of norms—of developing standards in this group. It seems obvious that there are differences in our individual styles, our personalities, and our ways of relating to each other. We, as a group, seem faced with certain questions about the world that we live in or want to live in—questions having to do with the rights of members, the need to be involved, the right not to become involved, and the right of calling on others. To what extent do we have the right or the obligation to put pressure on others? Similarly, to what extent does an individual have the right to decide for himself—that is, his own conditions of involvement? These are all matters having to do with the development of standards and norms. The incident that took place between John and several others is highly significant. How we come to grips with the issues of membership and control will probably continue to be important for us as a group. I wonder if anyone else has any thoughts on this?" (Group level, conceptual type, medium intensity.) The last few statements concentrate on stressing the development of standards and norms by encouraging the direct participation of members.

Intervention Outcome

This intervention focuses group attention not on whether a particular individual responds, but on the underlying group process and its relevance for the entire group. This may encourage an intensive discussion of the rights and responsibilities of membership, the "silent member," the acceptance of individual style, and control factors. This incident should allow group members to consider ways and means of utilizing the resources of each individual.

Optional Structural Interventions

4. Introspection, p. 211
5. Surrender and Support, p. 213
6. The Group Slap, p. 215

Critical Incident M-10: High-Risk Disclosure

Theme Topic: Sharpened Affects and Anxieties: Increased Defensiveness

Context of Incident

In the middle stages of group life the general climate has progressed to the point where one or more members are beginning to come forth with topics of an increasingly personal nature. These topics may involve intimate feelings among members or memories of the past emerging from one member. Those individuals who experience the greatest pressure from topics that are disturbing or those individuals whose life style is one of frankness and openness are usually the first to initiate this particular critical incident. Such a person has begun to speak to the group about past traumatic events, relating painfully honest feelings.

Event Preceding Choice Point

Alan (ending a long statement of his difficulties and fears centering on women and his related concerns about masculinity): "And so, that's why I get nervous in here around you, Jane, because you're female. I sweat when I wonder if the rest of the men will accept me—listen to what I say as important. I guess that's why I've acted like I have in this group: silent and sometimes angry in my answers . . . Well, that's where I am now, nowhere—and I don't know what else to say . . ."

The group remains silent, looking at Alan, slouched dejectedly in his chair.

Choice Point

This incident involves the issues of individual style, personal disclosure, and intimacy. It usually occurs when a group member "lets go too far" when

148

beginning to risk disclosure. If it occurs too quickly or prematurely, this situation will sometimes "freeze up" a group or inhibit other members from future personal exploration if the consequences of this member's revelation are not handled appropriately. The task of the group leader is to facilitate appropriate sharing in the service of both personal and group growth regarding disclosure.

What would you do at this point? Give rationale.

Suggested Intervention

Group Leader: "One of the areas of greatest concern and difficulty is the sharing of feelings in public. And certain people who feel more open or free or perhaps have problems that are increasingly heavy begin to share feelings earlier." (Group level, conceptual type, medium intensity.)

"Sometimes, I guess, Alan, you might feel you stand alone, because after you've shared your feelings, other members may tend to back off or be quiet or feel anxious. I guess that's pretty common, because many people identify with the person who is speaking. Perhaps it re-awakens old wounds that we all have. So there's that sense of awkwardness, of wondering how far this person will go, and—most frightening—how far will I go? This seems to be what's happening now." (Individual level, experiential type, medium intensity.)

"I guess some of us would prefer to ignore this sort of thing—but that's running away. I feel that if we never try to come to grips with people expressing their fears, then to that extent we hamper the growth of that person and thus of us all. I feel very touched by what Alan shared with us. I don't know if anyone else shared those feelings, but I'd like to hear what your feelings and thoughts are." (Group level, experiential type, medium intensity.)

This intervention provides a conceptual framework for looking at specific group responses and utilizes Alan's disclosure to deal with the impact on the group. The leader supports and encourages expressions of feelings and also recognizes the reactions of remaining members.

Intervention Outcome

This critical incident, if handled correctly, should serve as a prototype for all future expressions of feelings in a group setting by group members. Expressing feelings just for the sake of expressing feelings is not encouraged. Rather, the expression of feelings should be used to promote very specific goals for personal and group growth. Careful judgment on the part of the group leader is needed to prevent the group from either becoming an intensive psychotherapy group or encouraging members to open up who need more adequate self-controls. There would be no economy in endorsing or encouraging emotion without considering goals and criteria. The successful management of this incident may lead to an increase in the expression of direct feelings, both positive and negative, and the legitimization and support of personal concerns as they affect functioning in the group, as well as concerns centering on intimacy and group cohesion.

Optional Structural Interventions

5. Surrender and Support, p. 213
20. The Hand Press, p. 245

Critical Incident M-11: Revealing Feelings

Theme Topics: Norm Crystallization/Enforcement-
Defensification
Decreased Defensiveness and Increased
Experimentation

Context of Incident

This critical incident during the middle to end phases of group life deals with the control of emotions and the reactions to anxiety and tension in the group. It occurs when group members are sufficiently acquainted to risk personal disclosure and after they have established norms of defensification toward openness. Certain individuals appear to have a life style of rapid, high-risk disclosure. If such disclosure is not handled appropriately, it may inhibit the group. If it is handled appropriately, other group members can be encouraged to deal with emotion-laden material. In this instance, the disclosing member fulfills the function of a "model."

Event Preceding Choice Point

Barbara: "I used to be scared like this when I was close to people and yet I was afraid to draw away. Like the attraction I feel for some of the group members in here, and yet I'm afraid they will refuse me. When I was younger, I used to date men and even sleep with them because it seemed I was always on the verge of losing them. I feel the same way, with most of you, here and now. Like I might lose you."

A long silence follows the statement by Barbara, who has disclosed herself in a genuine expression of risk taking.

Choice Point

The group leader is faced with the need to support Barbara and at the same time facilitate emotional support and disclosure on the part of the rest of the group. This critical incident involves important issues of personal expression, group support, trust, and intimacy. There are some members who may be both threatened by and resentful of personal disclosure. It is important to respond in a manner that will facilitate group cohesion and solidarity and crystallize certain desirable norms in the group. The surface issue is a simple statement of individual position as well as the feelings reflecting that position. The major underlying issue involves the norm of risk taking through emotional expression.

What would you do at this point? Give rationale.

Suggested Intervention

Group Leader: "Let me share some thoughts with you. As Barbara was talking, I was thinking about some of the things she was saying and how they had meaning for my own life. And the more I began to think about them, the more I got a little uncomfortable. I guess that's because—I don't know about the rest of you—but I'm not sure I'm quite ready to share some of these things." (Individual level, experiential type, medium intensity.)

"As I looked around the room while she was talking, I noticed some of you were looking kind of uncomfortable and tittering. Obviously, there are a lot of mixed emotions, perhaps embarrassment and discomfort. I think it's pretty important because it involves some risks for Barbara to do this, that is, to share something of herself, especially where there hasn't been any reward for doing so. On the other hand, some of us may feel pushed back a little bit more as a result of this kind of disclosure, maybe feeling uncomfortable about possibly having to share things in this manner. So it's a double-edged sword with importance both to Barbara and to the group." (Group level, conceptual type, low intensity.)

"It seems to me, however, that there is only one direction we can go from here. And that's the direction of appropriate self-disclosure. I guess that's why we try to encourage and help each other disclose—not for the sake of disclosure, but for those materials and information that would be most helpful for learning and growth." (Group level, conceptual type, low intensity.)

The opening intervention statement established a mood that legitimized and supported Barbara's statements. At the same time, the implicit threat to other group members was recognized as a source of legitimate concern. The leader identified the likely mixed emotions of the other group members as well as their realistic self-concerns. Finally, the personal bias and value system of the group leader points to a direction or norm that would best encourage future group growth and development. In this instance, the genuine feelings of the leader were used in the service of the group.

Intervention Outcome

This intervention intends not to coerce all members into self-disclosing behavior, but to legitimize the expression of feelings, to experiment with more effective ways of interacting with others, and to encourage personal growth. The group leader will need to judge whether an individual needs to experiment with tighter or looser controls in order to function more effectively. Typically, in our society, a premium is placed on overcontrol, and the group leader may find many resistances to more flexible behavior patterns. There are times, however, when the group leader may wish to aid a group member in constructing firmer controls.

Optional Structural Interventions

5. Surrender and Support, p. 213
6. The Group Slap, p. 215
20. The Hand Press, p. 245

Critical Incident M-12: Verbal Battle

Theme Topic: Distributive Leadership

Context of Incident

This critical incident emerges over a period of time during the middle stages of group life when one or more group members consistently attack another group member or perhaps the group leader. This is usually reflected by an individual's "fight style" directed toward almost everyone. At times, the life style of constant battling may be evident from the very beginning of the group. Equally often, the life style may emerge only as the climate of the group becomes relaxed enough to encourage aggressive feelings. In either instance, this individual's continuous opposition must be handled in a manner that meets the perceived growth needs of both the individual and the group. The group is likely to regard the extent of its ability to handle an excessively aggressive member as an indication of growth. This pattern of aggressive, argumentative behavior may become so obvious that one or more group members comment directly on the interactions.

Event Preceding Choice Point

Charlie: "Do we have to do this exercise? Just sitting around like this bores me and makes me angry for wasting my time. If you're the leader, I want something better than this!"

Debbie: "Charlie, you know you've spent the last three sessions bitching and giving everyone hell. That makes me angry toward you. No matter what's said, you keep on fighting and dragging your feet!"

Ed: "Yeah, you've been doing this for a long time now, and without offering anything in return."

Silence follows this heated exchange, with all members concerned looking at each other in a strained, tense manner.

Choice Point

This incident involves the surface issue of Charlie's disagreeing with the leader, and Debbie's disagreeing with Charlie. Charlie's past history reveals a consistent pattern of aggressiveness toward nearly every group suggestion. His behavior seems to be based primarily on an overall personality trait rather than situational provocations by the group. The issues deal with a reaction to conflict and tension, with control, authority, and the rights of the individual vs. the rights of the group. Since it is assumed that Charlie's conflict with authority is part of a pervasive pattern in everyday life, this issue will be highlighted and emphasized.

What would you do at this point? Give rationale.

Suggested Intervention

Group Leader: "Can we stop for a minute, as a whole group, and try to get a picture of what's been happening? Let me ask you: Do you see what's been going on as just an issue between Charlie and Debbie? Do you see yourselves connected to it?" (Group level, experiential type, low intensity.) The leader identifies the specific process he believes to be important.

Frank: "Well, if I have to worry before I come in if it's going to hurt the other person, then I probably won't come in, because I don't know if it will help or hurt."

Group Leader: "How about the rest of you?"

Georgia: "Well, I kind of feel the same way. Should we be expressing what we feel, or just be concerned about the other person first?"

Hank: "I'd like to watch Charlie and Debbie slug it out."

Group Leader: "But what if it happens to people other than Charlie and Debbie? What if it happened to you, Hank, and you, Frank? What would you do? Would you want other people to come in and expand the area of discussion—or would you want more and more to be in the 'gladiator' position?" (Interpersonal level, experiential type, medium intensity.) This approach generalizes the issues and questions involved for consideration by other members.

Ivan: "Yeah, I'd like to learn how to help without accusing or condemning."

Group Leader: "How did you feel about your intervention, Charlie, the one you made before?" (Individual level, experiential type, low intensity.) This intervention brings the general issues into focus on the situation that precipitated the critical incident.

Charlie: "I guess I was more concerned with getting it off my chest than with helping anybody!"

Group Leader: "Yes, that's what I felt too. I suppose that's natural. I guess the main issue revolves around whether it's possible for somebody to express feelings and take part in differences without either being ignored or rejected. I don't think it's just Charlie. Unless we somehow figure out a way to help work with the Charlies, we're in trouble. And the job is more difficult since the Charlie-type reaction is that he doesn't typically communicate that he would really like any help. How about the rest of you? Do you want to try out some activities that might help us overcome some obstacles in working through the conflict we have?" (Group level, conceptual type, medium intensity.) Again the leader points out the problem and solicits help from the group.

At this point, the group leader might introduce a spontaneous theory input on individual life styles in a typical group; request group members to observe and identify various styles and their impact on the group here and now; or suggest that group members use their resources to prescribe more effective ways of functioning for those members whose life styles bring them into frequent conflict.

Intervention Outcome

This critical incident was an example of the many issues that may be embedded within a given situation. The context of the event and knowledge of the members involved suggested emphasizing the conflict over individual styles of behavior. Through the resolution of similar critical incidents, group members may develop the ability to work with, and utilize, the resources of all group members, even if there is initial conflict over behavior patterns. It is our bias that an effective group is able to function with a diversity of resources from group members who do not fit a common mold. (See Critical Incident B-17, Confronting Resistance, for a related instance. The surface issue seems the same in both instances—resistance to an activity suggested by the leader. However, in B-17, Ernie's opposition was generated by fear or threat to himself. At that stage of the group, there was no sense of distributed leadership; therefore, due to different underlying issues and the different maturity level, the incident was handled differently.)

Critical Incident M-13: Attacking the Leader

Theme Topic: Members Search for Position/Definition: Primary Group Transferences/ Countertransferences

Context of Incident

This critical incident, which occurs during the middle to end stages of group life, emerges from a group climate that encourages and supports confrontation. Full confrontation with the group leader usually occurs only after members themselves have become fairly comfortable in openly expressing their anger and conflict. Two or more members will frequently band together, usually with a spokesman, to comprise a faction that opposes the group leader. At the same time, this may split the group into two or more subgroups, one supporting the leader and the other opposing the leader.

Usually a high-intensity encounter, this incident is similar to Critical Incident B-19 and B-20. The latter incidents involve a one-to-one encounter between a group member and the leader, which erupts over a minor point or statement made by the leader. The present critical incident, by contrast, involves two or more members offering procedural criticisms of the leader which may polarize the group into two or more factions. Qualitatively, these two incidents involve different issues and concerns, although there is a degree of overlap.

Event Preceding Choice Point

Group Leader (concluding an intervention): "And so, I can see why you screamed at Frank when he cried."

Bill: "You know, you seem to be picking on Alice and Frank. It seems that others don't speak up—or don't discuss personal issues—and you don't even criticize them. I don't think that's right—or the way it should be handled. There are others who feel the same way."

Jack: "I agree with Bill."

Kathy: "I thought that, too."

Choice Point

The surface level is a disagreement between several group members and the leader. At a deeper level, there are issues dealing with control, authority, and leadership. These issues are seriously dividing the group, leading to at least one member's "testing for revolution." The subgroups that are emerging also represent the conflict at the points of friction. This event offers the opportunity to involve all members in conflict resolution, authority relationships, and responsibility for group direction.

What would you do at this point? Give rationale.

Suggested Intervention

Group Leader: "How do the rest of you feel? Are you bothered by this, too?" (Group level, experiential type, medium intensity.)

Matt: "I don't agree. I like what's been happening!"

Nancy: "Yeah, let's keep on this way."

Group Leader: "I was curious and wanted to find out who shares the same kind of feelings. What just happened isn't an isolated event, either. No more than what took place with Alice and Frank. In fact, I had the feeling that Bill was speaking informally for a subgroup here that shares certain feelings in common about me. And apparently there is another subgroup that doesn't agree with them. I'm not saying this in a wrist-slapping way, but rather to identify people who have a set of feelings in common. Would you buy that so far?" (Group level, experiential type, medium intensity.) While the immediate impulse may be to defend leadership actions, it is more appropriate to recognize and establish the group's feelings. This evaluation is communicated to the group members for their feedback.

Kathy: "Yeah, I think everybody feels a little bit of that."

Group Leader: "We've got an interesting kind of relationship here. We've got one subgroup that has some negative feelings about my leadership in this group, another that disagrees, and a few individuals who are vying for leadership or a relationship with me. What about the rest of you who haven't spoken up?" (Group level, conceptual type, medium intensity.) The leader attempts to sharpen the issues involved and to sound out the feelings of all other members.

Nancy: "Well, I'm confused. I don't know what to think."

Matt: "I don't know. Everybody seems to be talking and we don't seem to get anything done. It doesn't matter whether you're leading or he's leading. We never seem to get anywhere."

Group Leader: "I think what just went on in the last minute was probably the best example of what I have been trying to point out—that we have some serious lines that divide here. And one way to stop them is to get people involved in talking about them and how they feel about things that are going on. When we just come in with anger and criticism, without helping at the same time, it makes it very hard for people who have concerns to share them. I'd like to suggest an activity that might be of help here." (Group level, conceptual type, medium intensity, shifting to group level, structural type, high intensity. The shift occurs to facilitate group work in this area.)

Intervention Outcome

This critical incident attempted to point out and describe the properties of various subgroups that had formed. The ability to solve problems and determine direction revolves around members understanding the dynamics of their own group. The verbal interventions provided the appropriate setting for the structural intervention—an activity that could be used as a problem-solving technique in other groups.

Optional Structural Intervention

7. Group Observing Group, p. 217

Critical Incident M-14: Coming of Age

Theme Topic: Distributive Leadership

Context of Incident

This critical incident takes place in the middle to end stages of group life as members begin to fulfill more leadership functions and start to verbalize and to react with a heightened sense of responsibility and distributive leadership. The situation ends a long silence which has followed "pot-shot" comments on an important issue that the group would rather ignore than deal with directly.

Event Preceding Choice Point

Owen: "You know, each time we've started to talk about Helen's group participation, or absences, or contributions, we've started to back off."

Pam: "It seems to me that we may be afraid to hurt Helen. Is that holding us back?"

Choice Point

Here, the surface issue and underlying issue appear to be the same. A group member has assumed a leadership role and has shown effort, skill, and concern for the growth of the group. This is a desirable change and should be encouraged. It is also a sign that the group has progressed and is "coming of age." This critical incident deals with distributive leadership and/or group style as well as leadership-authority relations.

What would you do at this point? Give rationale.

Suggested Intervention

Group Leader: "I believe that what you just did was very important. You pointed out a couple of things that I think are crucial. By virtue of your observation you called our attention to a norm that has developed during the group—our reactions to personal pain and exposure. It can get very uncomfortable! And to handle it, the group calls on one of its members who is willing to serve in this connection because we know his service will be needed. That deals with one question, a normative one: Ought the group to continue working with one of its members? Is it a good thing or a bad thing?" (Individual level, conceptual type, medium intensity.)

"In another sense you were exercising what I think is a pretty important leadership function. You were not just giving an observation. What you did could have an impact on us as a group. We've talked about leadership in terms of functions; not simply personality traits or the position that a person has, but the functions that he or she performs that have an impact. So, clarifying, sharing observations, testing, confronting possible norms—these are all leadership functions. You did it last session, Owen, when you talked about whether or not the group had developed a style of quickly bandaging someone who might have been hurt. Do you remember? And that's the kind of thing that really begins to mark the level of mature growth of our group, when our members can perform these functions freely, so that we're all influenced by them. What do you think, Pam?" (Begins at individual level, conceptual type, low intensity, and shifts to group level, conceptual type, low intensity.)

Intervention Outcome

This flow from individual to group to individual level may accentuate the conceptual content of distributive leadership functions in a group and at the same time help the group and the individual who exercised leadership to see and understand better the positive effects of his behavior. This intervention may encourage other members to begin exercising distributive leadership functions.

END CRITICAL INCIDENTS

Critical Incident E-1: Acknowledging Hostility

Theme Topic: *Distributive Leadership*

Context of Incident

This critical incident occurs during the end phase of group life, as group members feel secure in the group and begin to look at their own personal styles and patterns of behavior as resources for group growth. Self-exploration and distributive leadership replace, in part, the leader's observations; and interdependence is established in recognizing the resources in both the group and the leader.

Event Preceding Choice Point

Arlette (to group leader): "I feel I'm getting hostile toward you again. I don't like what we're doing. And yet, I don't want to be this way. I don't want to be hostile toward what you have to tell me, but I don't know what to do."

Bart: "Yeah, I've noticed that you get hostile—several times before, particularly at the leader—but I don't know what to do."

Charlie: "I like you better when you don't come across hostile. I can understand what you are saying . . . "

Arlette (to leader): "My anger gets in the way of listening to what you say and I can't help getting mad. Everybody seems to tell me that."

Choice Point

The surface issue involves a group member's hostile feelings toward the leader. Underlying this issue are the more serious dynamics of interpersonal conflict resolution, counterdependent attitudes, and authority relations.

What would you do at this point? Give rationale.

Suggested Intervention

Group Leader: "Those are things I have felt take place every time you've gotten mad at me. I can almost see it developing. It's a kind of pick-up on some inconsistency that makes you angry. At a certain point you choose to let yourself become angry." (Individual level, experiential type, medium intensity.)

"At a certain point a person makes a choice to let himself get involved in a certain mood. You can feel it as a rising irritation. Do you all know what I'm talking about?" (Group level, conceptual type, low intensity.) This lets Arlette off the hook and gets other members involved to deal with the issue.

"You know at that point that you have already passed the choice point. But you can check it by saying, 'I'm starting to get angry with you because you are revealing a disappointment about me, my disappointment' or 'You're disappointing me again,' or others who see it can say, 'Cool it, Arlette.' But I do believe that people can make choices in terms of the moods they get in. You can come to possess and 'own' your own states of feelings—from the barely conscious level all the way to behavior and expression. At a certain point it is possible to exercise some control." (Group level, conceptual type, medium intensity.)

Bart: "You mean it's not always the feeling you change but the reaction to it."

Arlette: "That's it. You check your feelings before they get too far along the path. After a certain point you can't do very much with them."

Charlie: "You can, but it's more difficult since you have more invested."

This series of responses provides a resolution of the preceding event.

Intervention Outcome

These interventions, dealing with interpersonal conflict and control of deep personal emotions, may lead to further discussion of the related issues of control and spontaneity. This event, which demonstrates the ability of group members to analyze and understand the dynamics of their own behaviors, is a sign of the group's growth and maturity. Both skill and maturity are revealed in trying to discover and change existing behavior patterns.

Critical Incident E-2: Amending the Leader's Intervention

Theme Topics: Distributive Leadership
Group Potency

Context of Incident

Since this critical incident occurs in the end stages of the group, it carries quite different connotations from those at an earlier stage. By this time the group has usually effectively worked through authority issues surrounding the group leader's role. The climate of the group allows different members constructively to perform distributive leadership functions that can be accepted by other members and the leader.

Event Preceding Choice Point

Dick (following an intervention by the group leader, who may have partially missed the mark or some salient point in the just-finished process): "That's a good point. But it seems to me that what happened here was that John felt hurt when Bill said that to him. No one picked up on that fact, and I wonder why we ignored it."

Choice Point

This critical incident deals with a recognition of leadership and authority issues, especially as they involve group members who attempt to assume certain leadership functions. While on the surface level this critical incident represents a group member's attempt to facilitate group action, it has significance on a deeper level; at this phase of group life, a member is able to assume a leadership function and represent less of a challenge to the leader's authority and more of a permissible application of acquired skills for furthering constructive group movement.

What would you do at this point? Give rationale.

Suggested Intervention

There are two alternatives at this point, both of which should allow the initiated action ample time to develop its potential. The group leader's first alternative is to wait for John to respond to Dick's intervention. If John does not respond, the leader could support the request for feedback or information.

"You know, this makes a good deal of sense to me. I would like to hear, too. I think my comments were somewhat incomplete and off target. So, I would like to acknowledge and reaffirm Dick's observation of the limited nature of my intervention and to encourage a response to his question." (Couched within the framework of a group-level, experiential-type, low-intensity intervention is an individual-level, experiential-type, low-intensity intervention.)

Assuming the other members respond, the second alternative would be to intervene after the appropriate exchange has run its course. The purpose of this intervention would be publicly to reinforce the leadership functions Dick has demonstrated.

Group Leader: "I would like to comment on what happened in the last five minutes or so since I think it is quite exciting and significant. I think it represents a significant criterion for us to use in judging how far we have come since the beginning of our life as a group. I had made a comment about John that was followed by Dick's pointing out some additional things that could have been said. He evaluated and supplemented my intervention. In the early part of the group when members commented on or evaluated my interventions, I sensed, in part, a struggle with me as an authority. This time, however, I did not feel this way. I think we have worked through a number of these related issues and I see the kind of thing that Dick just did as representing a significant leadership function. His concern was not to challenge me but to add to the quality of my comments in such a way as to help other members of the group. And I think John benefited a great deal, as well as the rest of us. I am commenting on this now because it is just this kind of leadership behavior that I would like to reinforce. It makes it possible for me, and the rest of you, to contribute more openly and to learn from each other. This is, after all, an ideal outcome, to learn from each other." (Primarily group level, conceptual type, medium intensity.)

Intervention Outcome

This intervention calls attention to and reinforces the new process that has evolved and increases the likelihood of its future occurrence. It may tap dormant resources that can be pooled for more effective learning and facilitation of the growth and development of group members.

Critical Incident E-3: Withdrawal Symptoms

Theme Topics: *Distributive Leadership*
Group Potency

Context of Incident

It is close to the termination of the life of the group, with only a few sessions left. Up to this point all members have been sharing very deep, meaningful feelings and information about themselves. Now, a dramatic shift is evident. The members begin talking about light-hearted, irrelevant, or amusing things, as if deliberately to avoid further involvement on a personal level. This has continued for almost five minutes into the session. Finally one member who has expressed considerable sensitivity and empathy begins to speak.

Event Preceding Choice Point

Georgia: "You know something? I wonder why we're talking about all these things? It's almost like we're all withdrawing from the group!"

The group remains silent, considering its past behavior.

Choice Point

Both the surface and underlying issues have been recognized and dealt with by a group member. In doing this, Georgia is fulfilling the functions of a group leader—instilling in others the responsibility for distributive leadership. This is a sign of growth in the group.

What would you do at this point? Give rationale.

Suggested Intervention

Typically, at such times the group leader needs only to encourage members to express their feelings about the statement and one another.

Group Leader: "Georgia, could you share a bit more of your thoughts about that last statement?" (Individual level, conceptual type, low intensity.)

Georgia: "Well, it's like leaving a friend we love and we know we may never see again. Often, we try to drag out the good-byes, but sometimes we sort of withdraw from him, talk about silly things and try not to make the parting too emotional because that would be painful. We may be doing that now." (Group level, conceptual type, medium intensity.)

Group Leader: "I agree, Georgia. This might be a good place for us to explore the feelings we've been avoiding." (Group level, conceptual type, low intensity.)

Georgia: "I wonder if it might be a good idea, at this point, to share our perceptions of each other and allow everyone to have a chance to wind up any unfinished business?" (Group level, conceptual type, low intensity.)

Intervention Outcome

By the time a group reaches this stage in its group life, it will be able to profit from the suggestions of group members. Perhaps another member will start the feedback process, or a structural intervention may be suggested as a means of facilitating this interpersonal focus. The members are demonstrating skills of distributive leadership in a highly effective manner.

Optional Structural Interventions

8. Fantasy in Association, p. 219
14. Experiencing Closeness, p. 234

Critical Incident E-4: Must I Change?

Theme Topics: *Decreased Defensiveness and Increased Experimentation*
Group Potency

Context of Incident

During the beginning part of one of the final group meetings, the leader has just delivered a planned theory input (PTI), involving the feedback process and productive risk taking. One of the group members, who is highly intellectual and cognitively oriented, anxiously makes a statement directly to the leader.

Event Preceding Choice Point

Hank: "I've been sitting here listening to you and I wonder—are you talking about me? Am I supposed to change? What am I supposed to do? I've always been relatively secure the way I am. Why should I change—or how?"

In the silence that follows, all eyes are on the leader.

Choice Point

The surface issue involves responding to Hank's questions concerning the necessity for personal change. The more important underlying issue concerns the possibility of change, which, even in the most well-adjusted life style, is likely to produce some threat and anxiety. The problem that arises is that any suggestion of change is likely to be interpreted as an all-or-nothing affair. Care must be taken by the leader to address himself only to those behaviors capable of modification within the time limits and competencies of the group. The level of intervention for this particular critical incident should take into consideration both the issues involved in giving feedback, the benefits to both individual and group, and a means to link them both together.

What would you do at this point? Give rationale.

Suggested Intervention

The leader may choose to turn the question back to the group, answering as if the group had asked the question.

Group Leader: "Perhaps this is a question with which each of us is struggling. What do you, as a group, think and feel about Hank's question?" (Group level, experiential type, low intensity.)

While useful, this intervention may not take adequate advantage of the opportunity to integrate knowledge, values, and practical skills. It can be contrasted with a second alternative.

Group Leader: "Hank, I got the feeling as I was watching and listening to you just now that you were feeling pretty tense and uptight. The reason I mention it is that I feel that way, too, sometimes." (Individual level, experiential type, medium intensity.) This response communicates the leader's awareness of the feelings involved and his desire to be supportive.

"I guess the questions you raised, such as whether I can find a place for myself in the group, whether people are going to accept or reject me, how much I should risk revealing and how I can find out where I stand, are questions we all are struggling with, as a group." (Individual level, conceptual type, medium intensity.) This continuation points to the larger questions involved to which the leader wishes to sensitize the group.

"I wonder if the rest of you would share your feelings about this point?" (Group level, experiential type, high intensity.) This intervention deals directly with very important personal feelings. The group leader should allow the group members sufficient time to discuss their feelings concerning these issues before continuing.

"I would like us to consider some of the ways we stop ourselves from utilizing our full potential—not just in here, but in all groups. Perhaps it's a way we have of not listening, or of talking too much, or of talking too little, or of refusing to compromise. I feel we all know each other pretty well, right now, and we've invested a good deal of trust in the group. I'd like to suggest an exercise that may help us get at some of these questions and concerns." At this point, the leader may introduce a structural intervention entitled Behavior Prescription.

Intervention Outcome

This intervention was designed to suggest the possibility of improving the effectiveness of members in this and other groups, to introduce a skill exercise designed to pinpoint specific problem areas within each individual in a supportive atmosphere, to recommend and try out specific behavior prescriptions in the group for the remainder of the group's life, and to evaluate their effectiveness and receive supportive feedback.

This intervention may allow each member the opportunity to analyze his present mode of functioning within groups and to experiment with new, possibly more effective ways of functioning. If this exercise is conducted in an objective but supportive atmosphere, it is often one of the most valuable learning experiences encountered.

Optional Structural Intervention

22. Behavior Prescription, p. 249

Critical Incident E-5: Sexual Feelings

Theme Topic: Decreased Defensiveness and Increased Experimentation

Context of Incident

During the end stages of the group, cohesiveness, trust, and intimacy have progressed to the point that genuine feelings of closeness and intense affection have been fostered among members. Expression of genuine feelings has been realized, and the members are free enough to express intensely personal feelings toward each other.

Event Preceding Choice Point

Inez: "You know, after I had that encounter in the group with you yesterday? Well, I went home last night and I dreamed we were in bed together. I guess that just confirms what I've already told you about how I feel toward you."

Jack: "I'm glad you told me. I've been thinking a lot about us, too."

This interchange may be followed by positive expressions of intense affection among other group members.

Choice Point

This critical incident deals with membership and norm issues, especially regarding intimacy. At the surface level the members have progressed to an intimate level of personal expression. At a deeper level, members are feeling free enough to allow their own personal styles to emerge, especially in an area where people are typically slow to reveal themselves. The expression of intimate feelings toward each other is another step in the process of determining the extent to which these personal feelings are mutually shared, which may determine whether intimacy can progress and be established at a deeper level.

177

What would you do at this point? Give rationale.

Suggested Intervention

To foster the genuine and appropriate expression of feelings, the leader may respond in one of two ways. If this intense dialogue is followed by silence and a sense of discomfort, the initial intervention may be the following:

Group Leader: "You know, Inez and Jack, you were saying some pretty warm things to each other. You mentioned sexual relations and talked of your mutually shared intimate feelings toward one another. But, somehow, when you stopped, something happened in the group. Others didn't want to come in on their own and I'm not sure what the explanation for this is. However, two thoughts come to mind. On one hand, there is the possibility that the other members of our group didn't want to interfere in a kind of special fantasy world that you two had and were allowing it to exist without bursting the bubble by talking about themselves. On the other hand, maybe what you said to one another represents what a number of us have been thinking about each other. Certainly the subject of sleeping with someone—having sexual relations with a 'stranger'—is still generally taboo. Maybe we backed off from this subject. I wonder? Do we need to talk about it?" (Interpersonal level, experiential type, medium intensity.)

If the group members continue sharing their thoughts and intimate feelings about this topic and each other, a follow-up intervention might be:

Group Leader: "One of the big hang-ups that people ordinarily have is whether and how to get close to someone. We have struggled with both of these in the group. In growing up in our society emotions are often strained or filtered out of us. To some extent growing in this group represents a recapitulation of the processes we go through in our lives as a whole. So here we are again struggling with that question. On the part of Inez and Jack, we have witnessed a genuine and very loving expression of warmth without misinterpretation, without odious connotations. Other people have joined in and talked about similar feelings. It has created, for me, and I think for others, a sense of real good will, not a sense of phony cohesiveness that might block further group movement. However, the circle is not complete. Some of the rest of us may still have some unexpressed thoughts and actions. But this recent expression is a base for being able to deal even more honestly and usefully with the problems of relationships." (Group level, experiential type, medium intensity.)

Intervention Outcome

These interventions intend to encourage the free expression of genuine, personal, and appropriate feelings toward one another, as well as to promote a group atmosphere that receives these expressions with warmth and sincerity. If this atmosphere is accomplished, members may become less inhibited in realizing their own partially suppressed individual styles. A greater group cohesiveness may be achieved along with a more honest and useful approach to dealing with problems of interrelationships.

Optional Structural Interventions

23. Hear My "I," p. 251
24. Last Impression, p. 253

Critical Incident E-6: Creative Risk Taking

*Theme Topic: Decreased Defensiveness and
Increased Experimentation*

Context of Incident

This critical incident, occurring during the last sessions before the group is to terminate, has been preceded by various members specifying the ways in which they would like to change their behavior. Members have expressed wishes to become more aggressive or less aggressive or more tactful or more supportive, etc. There has been an increasing emphasis on trying out new behavior and experimenting with new ways of relating to other group members. Up to this point, however, there have been only a few tentative attempts at creative risk taking—trying out the behavior in front of the group. There is also a mild undercurrent of awkwardness and anxiety, in spite of the supportive atmosphere that is present.

Event Preceding Choice Point

Karl, an older group member who was a career Army officer, spoke of his intense desire to learn to listen and to display feelings with his family. The nature of his duties, he believed, prevented any show of emotion. Unfortunately, this conditioning over the years was now preventing him from exhibiting the deep, warm feelings he had for those outside his command. During this session Karl sat tensely in a ramrod position in his chair until Maureen, another older group member, began sharing some emotionally moving stories of her childhood loneliness. Tears were observed in Karl's eyes. He quietly rose and went over to Maureen's chair and held her hand quietly. The other members of the group became silent and looked surprised by this unexpected and atypical behavior. Silence continued for about twenty seconds.

Choice Point

The issue for the leader, at this point, is whether to remain silent or to comment on what has just happened. He will have to make a careful judgment. If he does not intervene at all, he may miss the opportunity to reinforce and compliment Karl for taking a creative risk and showing his feelings in an appropriate situation and to encourage others to experiment with new behavior, using Karl as an example. However, an ill-timed or inappropriate intervention may break the mood of close interpersonal sharing and intimacy. At times, it is enough to sit quietly, hoping that other group members will come forth (which they usually do), while at other times a gentle prod is needed.

What would you do at this point? Give rationale.

Suggested Intervention

Group Leader: "Karl, I want to let you know how much I appreciate what you just did. I feel very warm and close to you, not just because you went to someone who needed you, but because you responded on a genuine, warm, emotional level—something you had trouble doing before." (Individual level, experiential type, medium intensity.)

Intervention Outcome

This intervention may result in supportive statements from other group members as well as increased motivation among all members to experiment with new behaviors on their own. In this critical incident, the intervention intended to minimize disruption of the prevailing mood of the group. It was purposely an experiential type since a conceptual type would probably have detracted from the mood. Following this incident, an increase in group cohesion would be expected.

Optional Structural Interventions

Critical Incident E-7: Growth or Therapy?

Theme Topic: Group Potency

Context of Incident

This critical incident usually occurs as a reaction to conflict and tension in the end stages of group life. It involves a group style of reassurance to prevent further painful exposure by a specific group member. This stems from a realistic sense that further exploration might not be productive for the individual or for the group. This incident usually emerges when a group member becomes increasingly upset while relating personal concerns.

Event Preceding Choice Point

Bill: "So, like I just told you, I don't feel that I'm worth too much as a man or as a person. I have serious doubts and fears about my manhood."

Nancy: "Well, I think you've done a great deal for this group. You were supportive and strong when others were weak and needed help. And there's no reason for you to think that you are anything but important and special in our group."

Other members continue the conversation with further abstract intellectualizations.

Choice Point

The surface issue here involves self-disclosure. How personally and deeply does a group involve itself? Underlying this question are issues of intimacy and feelings of inadequacy and the question of to what extent the group should focus on deep-seated personal problems. Some members, no doubt, feel that further expression would be too much for the person disclosing his feelings, or that the disclosure might inhibit the forward movement of the group. If this event had happened in the early stages of group life, the supportive comments by other group members would be seen as defensive maneuvers motivated by anxiety. The leader must judge whether group members are attempting to alleviate their own anxiety by "closing up" Bill or whether the observed interaction is appropriate to his needs. The former situation is known as "red-crossing" and is more likely to occur in the early phases of the group. (See Critical Incident B-32, Red-Crossing.) Here the members seem to have evaluated the situation correctly and are appropriately supporting Bill to prevent further unnecessary pain. As such, it is an indication of group growth.

What would you do at this point? Give rationale.

Suggested Intervention

Group Leader: "You know, Bill has talked a lot about his own sense of anxiety and insecurity, and how, in certain ways, he doesn't think very much of himself. A number of you have commented reassuringly that he has been a good member, that he's not worthless, and that he is not deserving of such low self-esteem. This has had the effect, and I assume it's an intended effect, of closing a wound, of stopping further pain on Bill's part." (Group level, experiential/conceptual type, medium intensity.) This response effectively summarizes the just-finished process.

The group leader continues: "I agree that this is important to communicate to Bill. I think it is important for each of us to feel his own membership in the group, so that we don't feel isolated and alone. I wonder, though, if there is more than that message in what some people have been saying to Bill. I wonder if in addition to saying, 'Bill, we love you. We care for you. Don't think so ill of yourself,' I wonder if we aren't also saying, 'Maybe you ought to hold off right now. Maybe you ought to reflect on what you've said and the responses of others, a little, and maybe you ought not to open up completely right now. There will be other opportunities for self-exploration, so don't pour everything out completely right now.' I wonder if we're not saying that to him?" (Group level, conceptual type, medium intensity.) This response reflects the process of what has been going on and gets Bill off the hook.

"Sometimes, in the interest of growth and for the best of intentions, a person may need to be encouraged to slow down in order to do some thinking about what has been said. I think it is important for us to talk about these observations, because they represent some pretty crucial questions for us: Do we say things directly? Do we not only express positive feelings, but do we try also to comment on the impact a person is having, particularly when the person is obviously in pain? If so, what do we do about it? I'm hoping we can talk about this in an effort to build up our explicit standards regarding this issue. What do you think?" (Group level, conceptual type, low intensity.) Here a spontaneous theory input is followed by an attempt to open the discussion to the group.

Intervention Outcome

This intervention lets the group see how it has dealt with an intense disclosure by one of its members. By discussing the different behaviors of several members, the group may see the relevance for the entire group. The intervention underscores the bias that complete and uncontrolled personal disclosure may not be the most desirable or healthy act. There are times when the best way to help an individual is to supply standards or controls he can use in managing his behavior. An effective group can help its members "let it all hang out" and, equally important, "tuck it all in" when necessary.

Optional Structural Intervention

16. Affection Blanket, p. 237

Critical Incident E-8: Taking Responsibility

Theme Topic: Group Potency

Context of Incident

This critical incident occurs during the end stages of group life, when a group has developed a norm of *not* talking about task issues and is focusing almost entirely on feelings and intimacy issues. During the middle of a personal disclosure by one group member, another group member asks a totally irrelevant question, reflecting no awareness of the feelings involved. It might be an attempt on the part of the member to shift the focus of the group to another issue.

Event Preceding Choice Point

Owen: "I have been very much concerned with the fact of death and dying. I've been afraid of it all my life and I feel particularly alone since my father died not too long ago. And I've really been afraid in here that I'm going to lose some people that I'm particularly fond of . . . "

    Pat: "I wonder if we could discuss the party we're supposed to have so we could start making some plans for refreshments and entertainment."

    Rhoda: "How can you talk of something like that after what he just said!"

    Sarah: "Didn't you hear what he said? How can you completely ignore his feelings? Don't you care about him at all?"

    Tom: "Did what he said about death make you anxious, Pat?"

Choice Point

The surface issue is clear: a group that has focused on emotional issues and given minimal attention to task issues resists leaving someone's feelings "up in the air." Underlying issues deal with dissenting members, the rules of membership, and group norms. The underlying issues concern the group's style in dealing with anxiety-provoking situations and the group's sense of responsibility for others, as well as group potency and accountability for what people do to each other.

What would you do at this point? Give rationale.

Suggested Intervention

The group may handle the situation, since members have developed some skills and potency in diagnosis. If this occurs, the group intervention might go as follows:

Vicki: "I'm feeling uncomfortable right now, because after Owen said a hell of a lot about himself, Pat made some comments about the party. That made me do a double-take because I didn't know what to do with Pat's statement. I wonder if anyone else is feeling at a loss, or frustrated, or maybe angry? I don't know. How do you feel?" (Group level, experiential type, medium intensity.) This response summarizes the ongoing process and invites discussion by other members.

Walt: "Pat, are you surprised at the comments that have just been directed to you? Are you aware of the feeling that people are trying to communicate to you about your having made an irrelevant response to Owen and disregarded his feelings?" (Individual level, experiential type, medium intensity.) Walt's comments are apparently intended to get Pat to collect his thoughts about what just happened, how the group used him as a target, and why.

Walt may continue with another individual-level, experiential-type, medium-intensity intervention to get Pat more deeply involved as well as to connect him to Owen.

Walt: "Was it that you weren't concerned? Or was it that you were *too* concerned?"

If Pat or other members do not respond to this interaction, the leader may say:

"You know, Pat, sometimes people seem to be very uninterested on the surface when actually they are so concerned and so linked to what's happening to another person that it is actually painful. Sometimes even they are not aware that they may be changing the topic to a less painful one to block pain from themselves." (Individual level, conceptual type, medium intensity.) "Did Owen say some things that kind of got you uptight?" (Individual level, experiential type, medium intensity.) This shift in intervention type should help the person comment on his feelings in this situation by giving him conceptual material to use and yet maintain the emotional involvement to foster increased communication.

Intervention Outcome

This intervention was described in two distinct stages, depending upon the ability of the group to recognize and deal with a significant group event as it emerged. The first choice allowed the group to report the event and evaluate it and to respond to Pat. If this intervention was ineffective or inappropriate, a second conceptual intervention was offered, by the leader. This general approach allows the group to assume more responsibility for analyzing and understanding its own behavior, with less direction needed by the group leader. It is important to note that Pat was not directly challenged or castigated; rather, he was offered a description of his behavior along with several questions regarding possible motives for his actions. Other members were encouraged similarly, via feedback. This critical incident is a good opportunity to present appropriate models of feedback.

Critical Incident E-9: Back-Home Applications

Theme Topic: Termination

Context of Incident

This critical incident has been preceded by some discussion attempting to relate the learnings of the group experience to significant others in life. One group member, who has been encouraged to overcome his shyness and feelings of unease in social situations, is in the process of graduating from school and looking for permanent employment.

Event Preceding Choice Point

Jerry: "I was really wondering just now, as I have for the last several days, what effect this program may have when I get a job, because some of the things that have been encouraged in here will get you into trouble outside . . . I mean, you can get stepped on for being too honest, or open, or trusting, can't you?"

Choice Point

Both the surface and underlying issues are apparent and congruent: a group member is concerned that the knowledge, skills, and values acquired in the group either will not be applicable to the real world or will be detrimental to success. This is a realistic concern and an issue that should involve all of the group members. In essence it involves the issue of re-entry and application of group principles.

What would you do at this point? Give rationale.

Suggested Intervention

Group Leader: "Jerry, I'm glad you brought that up. I think it's probably an issue that concerns all of us. It's the problem of 'How do we apply what we've learned in the group to the outside world?' In another way, we're asking, 'What behaviors are appropriate in what situations?' Is that how the rest of you see it?" (Group level, conceptual type, low intensity.)

Kathy: "Yeah, I'm reminded of the movie *Bob & Carol &Ted & Alice,* and the disastrous attempts to apply love and trust and openness to everyone."

Marian: "But where does it say we're 'supposed to' or 'have to' do that? It seems to me that if I have acquired any real capacity for trust or love, I'm going to be a much more complete—yes, even human—person when I come across the right person or persons and the right place."

Lennie: "Yeah, now at least I know what I'm capable of, with the right people and setting. Now, I'm more ready to be open with others."

Group Leader: "I think we all know that there are many inappropriate places to exhibit our learnings from this group: inappropriate because the circumstances hinder rather than facilitate common human interaction. It's a pretty rough analogy, but it's like finally discovering what love is like and how good you are with it. I hope we don't then go showering it indiscriminately on everyone, whether they are willing to accept it or not." (Group level, conceptual type, low intensity.)

Nancy: "It's just that you respect other life styles—even those based on values different from yours. If you're different as a result of this group, well, fine and great—let enough show through, and, under the right circumstances, others will react differently toward you."

This sharing dialogue can be augmented by a role play to focus on specifically designated areas in which any member anticipates difficulty.

Intervention Outcome

All group members may participate in a discussion of this issue, offering their insights and support to each other. However, supportive discussion is not adequate without delineating specific situations in an attempt to understand what, when, and how to apply the insights and skills derived from the group.

Optional Structural Interventions

22. Behavior Prescription, p. 249
24. Last Impression, p. 253

Critical Incident E-10: Group Values vs. Organizational Values

Theme Topic: Termination

Context of Incident

This event occurs during the latter period of group life when the mood has been established for sharing, support, and intimacy. In the past, the leader, from time to time, has stressed the importance of trying new behaviors, of attempting new experiences and more productive methods of interaction. During this session, one of the older group members has been looking very hurt and pained.

Event Preceding Choice Point

George (in a strained voice): "I've tried hard to utilize many of the observations and the learnings I've acquired in here in the outside world. But I'm working for an organization that is very conservative and straitlaced and that steps on any individual expression along these lines. By constantly trying out these new behaviors, I've just about put my job on the line. I really wonder what to do about this!"

A few members attempt to offer some help, but with little success. Finally the group falls silent.

Choice Point

Several issues are involved here. One is the transfer of group learning to the back-home situation. A second is the issue of what values are a part of the group and what values may be apart from it. Another basic issue is the extent of responsibility of the group for helping this individual.

What would you do at this point? Give rationale.

Suggested Intervention

The first choice might be to remain silent in order to allow group members to handle this problem. However, this is an important choice point involving a number of issues that are vital not only to the individual involved, but to the successful conclusion of the group. Perhaps a good measure of the maturity of a group is the extent to which it is able to apply its potent resources to aid a member who seeks help. If the group is unable to help this member adequately, the group leader may make a brief conceptual intervention followed by a structural intervention.

"I feel what George is saying about his own life, and the attempts to apply what we have been learning and experiencing in here goes beyond George and includes all of us. I think this would be a good occasion for us as a group to try to be of specific help." (Group level, conceptual type, low intensity.)

"Let me suggest that we break up into quartets and take about thirty minutes or so to give each person an opportunity to get help in applying the group's values to his situation as well as George's. When we come back, perhaps we can share some of these, try to pull together some of the common concerns and directional signals that could give us some guidelines." (Group level, structural type, medium intensity.)

The subgroups should attempt to discuss the problem as specifically as possible. When all subgroups reconvene, both support and specific concrete help should be encouraged from the other members toward George.

Intervention Outcome

There are a number of reasons for this particular type of intervention. It focuses the group on an implicit question almost all groups develop sooner or later, i.e., "What is the relationship of our behavior in the group to the back-home situation?" Also, discussion of this common group problem adds an element of emotional cohesion and group support, regardless of its outcome: emotional support that a member such as George can take with him into his back-home situation. It brings about the chance for members who have experienced the same problem to give specific, concrete individual advice to George and others. Finally, it opens up the entire area of "re-entry into the real world" as a topic of importance and concern for all. This procedure will help facilitate the termination phase and promote the generalization of many of the group concepts and learnings back into the "real world."

Optional Structural Interventions.

22. Behavior Prescription, p. 249
24. Last Impression, p. 253

Critical Incident E-11: Final Focus

Theme Topic: Termination

Context of Incident

This critical incident occurs in the last three or four group sessions. It arises out of a context in which most of the group work has been completed. Various group members have even begun contrasting first impressions with some present impressions of each other. It is during this time that the group leader may wish to suggest an especially effective and involving structural activity that will help provide satisfying closure for everyone. Thus, this intervention may arise from a specific set of circumstances and a receptive atmosphere, rather than any specific statements or behaviors by group members.

Event Preceding Choice Point

Generally, there are "finishing-up" or "wrapping-up" statements by one or more group members, all of which occur toward the end of the group's life. What apparently is needed at this point is some means of focusing the entire group's attention on one member at any given time, thereby enabling the members to receive maximum feedback, if the natural process of feedback and interaction requires augmentation.

Choice Point

The issue here is whether to continue to allow group members to interact sporadically with each other as the group nears its end as a group or to provide a means that will further focus intense and potent feedback for all members. The group leader should evaluate the importance of the ongoing process before he utilizes any specific intervention: it may well be that the group is more satisfied using its own method of progression.

What would you do at this point? Give rationale.

Suggested Intervention

Group Leader: "I'd like to suggest a structured experience that would not have been possible or successful earlier in the life of the group. But now we trust and care for each other and can listen more closely and perceptively to the feedback we receive from each other. The activity goes as follows: in the middle of the room we place a chair. Whenever a volunteer sits in the chair, we all have a responsibility to give that person feedback in three basic steps. First, we give him our fantasies as to how he comes across, e.g., a rock, a tree on top of a mountain, a river, etc. Second, he leaves the room for five minutes during which everyone discusses his life style and we prepare specific behavior prescriptions. At the end of five minutes, he returns to the chair and receives all feedback quietly, without responding. At the end he may ask specific questions or respond in any way he wishes. Then another person takes the chair, and so on." (Group level, structural type, medium intensity.)

Intervention Outcome

This intervention may allow each group member sufficient feedback in order to achieve satisfying personal closure. It should not be forced on the group, and no one should be made to participate even if the group decides to use the exercise. Specific attention should be given to the need to explore or discuss the feedback until the member feels satisfied and closure has been accomplished. To prevent frustration and premature closure, at least fifteen minutes should be allowed for each group member.

Optional Structural Intervention

23. Hear My "I," p. 251

Critical Incident E-12: Impacting the Real World

Theme Topic: Termination

Context of Incident

This event occurs during the last few sessions before termination of the group. The members have been discussing the application of the skills and knowledge gained in the group to the outside world. Some of their discussion has centered about humanitarian concerns. One group member, who has been relatively silent and somewhat inclined to withdraw passively when faced with opposition and conflict, enters the discussion.

Event Preceding Choice Point

Fred: "I've been thinking about the difficulties I've been having with my job for quite some time now. I work in a detention home, part-time, as you know. I just can't get over how they push those kids around, like caged animals. If I were to say anything, they would just ignore me or give me a rough time."

Gloria: "What do you usually do?"

Fred: "Oh, I don't know. I guess I just bottle it up or withdraw . . . I usually withdraw."

Choice Point

The potent surface issue here is how group members can apply the learnings and skills involved in working with others on real-world problems. An underlying issue with this particular group member is his life style of withdrawing instead of applying his personal resources to the job. Both of these issues may be brought out, at this point, since the group has progressed to the point of dealing openly with life styles and helping individual members.

What would you do at this point? Give rationale.

Suggested Intervention

Group Leader: "Fred, how are you feeling right now?" (Individual level, experiential type, low intensity.)

Fred: "Well, frankly, I'm feeling frustrated, helpless and caught."

Gloria: "Fred, what paths or alternatives do you have in your job situation?"

Fred: "Well, I guess I could become more aggressive or withdraw."

Group Leader: "What do you typically do—and does it make you happy or satisfied?" (Individual level, conceptual type, low intensity.)

Fred: "Yeah, I see what you mean. My old life style of running away again. No—it makes me sad and miserable."

Gloria: "I see another choice: sticking with it and doing as much as you can in a humane way. All within the limitations of your job. Do you have any specific people or situations that give you trouble? If so, let's deal with them now—how about role playing?"

Fred: "Well, O.K. That might give me some suggestions for more satisfying responses."

Intervention Outcome

Role playing or additional dialogue between Fred and other group members should continue until specific concrete advice and help is rendered. The individual should also be allowed to practice and experiment with any proposed new behavior until he feels comfortable. He should be encouraged to "try out" his new behavior in his job situation in a gradual and realistic progression. Difficulties should be reported back to the group as feedback, so that minor modifications may be introduced to enhance effectiveness for this individual.

Optional Structural Intervention

22. Behavior Prescription, p. 249

Critical Incident E-13: Closure

Theme Topic: Termination

Context of Incident

This event occurs during the final group session. Group members have generally finished saying their good-byes and the atmosphere is one of resignation and sadness. In general, all the unfinished business has been completed and there is a reluctance to stay and yet a greater reluctance to break up the group and leave. The majority of the group members are quiet and contemplative, feeling a sense of intimacy and yet not really knowing how to express the sensation of "oneness" with the group.

Event Preceding Choice Point

The group's behavior is generally one of mild sadness and depression. Occasionally, a few sighs are heard or someone makes an attempt to tell a joke which does not go over well. There are typically long periods of silence that precede this particular intervention by the group leader.

Choice Point

The issue, in this final group session, is how to assist the group members in saying their good-byes in the most significant and meaningful manner possible. Otherwise, the final session may be nonproductive and end on an unnecessarily depressed note. A suggested strategy is the use of a structural intervention that deals directly with group expression of emotion.

What would you do at this point? Give rationale.

Suggested Intervention

Group Leader: "It's always hard to say good-bye. Especially to people we've grown quite close to. I don't really know of any way of saying it that can escape the sadness. I'd like to suggest something at this point that may help us to say good-bye in a meaningful way to all of us." (Group level, experiential type, low intensity.) The leader then suggests a structural intervention to focus and resolve these feelings.

"I'd like for each of us to close our eyes for about one minute and get in touch with our feelings about ourselves and each other. At the end of a minute, I'd like us to get up slowly, with our eyes still closed, move about the room, and simply do whatever we feel like doing—all without talking. Let's just see how we all end up, without planning or thinking or talking. O.K., let's close our eyes . . . " (Group level, structural type, medium intensity.)

Intervention Outcome

This structural intervention leads group members to stand up and wander about until they come into contact with one another and finally form clusters that ultimately unite into groups. The groups usually stand silently together for a while, holding hands or embracing. Frequently they will be observed swaying together or singing together. Finally, after an appropriate period of time, the group leader may ask all members to open their eyes and look at the small society that has been formed. The group leader may then ask all members to express their good-byes in verbal or nonverbal ways and to leave when they have finished. This is usually a satisfying way to resolve and terminate the group.

Introduction to Structural Interventions

Structural interventions have long played an important role in growth groups, especially in encounter groups. Many have evolved through adaptation to fit the specific needs of particular groups and/or leadership styles. The twenty-four structural interventions in this section have been chosen for their usefulness in augmenting the verbal interventions used in the critical incidents.

Determining the originators of these exercises is difficult; however, whenever possible the authors have attempted to give credit to the earliest source of the exercises described.

Major contributors in this area include Schutz (1967)[1] and Gunther (1968, 1971),[2] both presently at Esalen Institute. Group leaders working with the National Training Laboratories[3] have developed and/or adapted exercises to fit the specific needs of laboratory training. Fritz Perls (1969) used structural interventions extensively in Gestalt therapy, and J. L. Moreno (1959) is the pioneer of role-playing exercises using psychodrama techniques. Pfeiffer and Jones (1969-1975) are responsible for disseminating a large body of useful structured experiences.

The reader is referred to these sources for a wide range of structural interventions, which may be used in conjunction with verbal interventions, as demonstrated in this manual, and which may be classified by means of the Intervention Cube. (See Chapter 3 in the text.)

---

[1]Variations of fourteen of these exercises (1, 2, 3. 5, 8, 12, 13, 14, 15, 16, 17, 18, 19, and 24) are found in William Schutz, *Joy: Expanding Human Awareness*, New York: Grove Press, 1967. Descriptions used in this text appear with the permission of the author and publisher.

[2]Six of the exercises utilized in this text (4, 5, 6, 16, 20, and 23) were pioneered by Bernard Gunther at the Esalen Institute, and variations can be found in his works. For descriptions see Bernard Gunther, *Sense Relaxation Below Your Mind*, New York: Macmillan, Collier Books, 1968, and *What to Do till the Messiah Comes*, New York: Macmillan, Collier Books, 1971. Permission has been granted by author and publisher for use in this text.

[3]Three of these exercises (7, 11, and 21) were the products of work at National Training Laboratories/Institute for Applied Behavioral Science and are used in this text with permission from Learning Resources Corp./NTL.

Structural Interventions

1. EMPATHIC COMMUNICATION
(B-1, B-3, M-2)

When

"Pairing" activities[1] may be effective interventions in dealing with a number of dynamics, i.e., conflict resolution, trust and intimacy, and/or individual styles of communication such as intellectualizing. If two members are having difficulty in either acknowledging and expressing their feelings to each other or in accepting the feeling or position of the other, the group leader can choose to follow the verbal with the nonverbal interaction in the communication dyad.

How

Group Leader: "For the past ten minutes or so, we have sat on the sidelines watching you, Jim and Mike, attempt to express how you are feeling toward each other. It seems you are having some difficulty both in saying exactly what you are feeling and in hearing what the other person is saying. I wonder whether you would try something which might help you, and us, too, to understand a little better what each is saying? O.K.? Good. First, it probably would be helpful if the two of you exchange chairs and face each other. Now, I want you to try to state as clearly and specifically as possible what you heard the other person saying to you. I think it is important that you try to get into his shoes and express as honestly as possible the other's position and 'feelings.'"

The focus is on empathic understanding and the reasonableness of the "opposition." This intervention could then be followed by nonverbal communication of the other's position, particularly if either tends to intellectualize or fumble for words to express feelings.

---

[1]See W. C. Schutz, *Joy: Expanding Human Awareness*, New York: Grove Press, 1967, pp. 137-140, for a related exercise, "The Non-Verbal Dyad." This description appears with the permission of author and publisher.

Results

Even if the two are not successful in exchanging places and viewpoints, the benefit of this method can still be maintained by asking what fantasies or pictures immediately come to mind. People usually have an immediate image that they can identify. "If you had felt free to express yourself, what do you think would have happened?" or "As you tried to visualize this exercise, what came to mind?" In both methods it is very helpful first to ask the adversaries to sit facing each other, in direct physical confrontation. The close physical proximity in addition to the instructions usually promotes faster, more effective bonds of understanding and closeness between the participants.

Thus, this intervention may be used with a conflict between two members, or it may be used to draw all group members closer together. In this last utilization, the entire group divides up into pairs. One member of each pair is to spend five minutes telling his partner, nonverbally, what he feels is "most significant" about himself. Following this ten-minute period of time, the other partner takes a turn. When all members of the group reassemble, both members of the pair may then discuss their feelings about this exercise, each reporting on his "understanding" of the other. This procedure promotes a faster sense of acquaintance and intimacy than would occur if members sought out superficial information, as they might be inclined to do.

2. EARLY PERCEPTIONS
   (B-1, B-3)

When

This intervention is preferably used at the beginning of group life.[1] It is often profitable also to use Last Impression as the final structured experience of the group to illustrate the changes that have taken place in the perceptions of any given individual, since the beginning stages of group life. This experience is designed to illustrate the various individual cues people use in trying to become acquainted with others.

How

In everyday interactions people often relate to each other by unconsciously picking up verbal and nonverbal cues in an effort to categorize or pigeonhole other persons. In other words, people take short cuts in getting acquainted by reacting in a stereotyped way to initial cues. At the beginning of a group, the leader may suggest a way of exploring this process by having each member stand and face the group and receive feedback from the rest of the group as to how the group sees this member.

Next, each person may be asked to give his impressions of each of the other group members, not only verbally, but also by standing directly in front of the person to get a much more direct awareness of his presence, looking him straight in the eye so that his attention is more easily directed to the person, and touching him in whatever way best expresses the feelings of the "toucher," while he describes his impression of the "touchee." This procedure makes the reality of the other person much greater.

---

[1] W. C. Schutz, in *Joy: Expanding Human Awareness*, New York: Grove Press, 1967, pp. 126-127, suggests a variation of this exercise, called "First Impression," for beginning groups: giving feedback on appearance before any verbal communication begins in the group. This description appears with the permission of author and publisher.

Results

While raising the anxiety level of group members, this exercise usually produces an emotional bond between both the giver and the receiver of feedback. In the context of our culture, which tends to view touching as related to sex and aggression, touching may evoke more tension than the verbal exchange.

The discussion following this experience may cover the question of "How does one relate to people and what are the feelings involved?" Questions may focus on both the individual and the group. The above verbal approach should be used with caution as it may "freeze up" group members and become too threatening to be productive. While experienced group leaders may be able to work productively with the anxiety generated, less-experienced group leaders may wish a less-demanding approach. In this latter situation, each group member is requested to write down, in a few sentences or so, his "early perceptions" of each of the other group members. When finished, each member puts the impressions away in his notebook or in a file which he must not look into until the end of the group. At that time he then compares his "early perceptions" with his "last impressions," and the cues that determined his statements in each case. Group sharing, at this time, is likely to be a personally informative event for all group members involved.

If, in the judgment of the leader, it would not be too threatening, each member can collect the written impressions about himself (signed or unsigned) and read them aloud. There is no pressure on members to discuss these judgments, but the leader gives his support if members wish to do so.

3. THE SHARING PROGRESSION
(B-1, B-5)

When

This intervention may be used at any stage, but it is most useful in the beginning stages to break down interpersonal mistrust and resistance and to promote acquaintance among members.[1] Following the dyad, or two-person group, the smaller groups may be enlarged in successive steps to four, eight, etc., until finally the entire group is back together after a programmed intimacy encounter.

How

To facilitate individuals in freely expressing their feelings, group members may be paired in any number of ways. Each dyad usually meets for ten to fifteen minutes, but this varies with the leader. The partners may be asked to face each other or one partner is asked to sit behind the other and just listen as the first shares the most important aspects of himself. Then the partners reverse positions. One variation is for the two to develop an interchange of intimate sharing. The leader's instructions are focused on providing conditions for genuine expression and understanding to take place upon which a relationship can be formed.

Group Leader: "In many situations in the community we become acquainted with other people by giving and receiving 'insurance data,' i.e., where were you born, where do you work, etc., or by talking about similar interests (football, art, school). If this is the extent of our sharing, I wonder how well we ever really get to know each other? I'd like us to divide into dyads and see whether in here we can both express and hear the important parts of ourselves we want to share with each other. While one partner shares, the other listens. Then positions are reversed. After this procedure, each may want to share his feelings about what his partner has said."

---

[1]A related exercise, "The No-Exit Dyad," is described by W. C. Schutz in *Joy: Expanding Human Awareness*, New York: Grove Press, 1967, pp. 75-78. This description appears with the permission of author and publisher.

Following the dyad meeting, it has been found productive to bring two dyads together, forming a group of four people, and to give them the same instructions as above. In this manner, groups of two are made into groups of four, and so on, until the entire group is again reformed on a more trusting and freer interpersonal level.

Results

The results are usually quite productive when followed by a discussion of "What topics were introduced first?" or "How did each one feel?" or "How does the group feel now toward each other, as compared with before the exercise?" This is also an excellent way to introduce to the group the concepts of group trust, intimacy, and cohesion, and it may serve as a modeling foundation for future behavior. This situation is unique in that participants, according to the rules of the game, are urged to maintain the relationship and not follow the usual pattern of defensiveness or withdrawal from a difficult situation. Having this successful experience enhances the potential for coping with resistances to disclosure and increases confidence in one's ability to follow through an interpersonal situation to a successful outcome.

4. INTROSPECTION
(B-4, B-24, B-25, B-26, B-29, M-9, E-6)

When

This is an excellent beginning structured experience[1] designed both to "warm" the participants to forthcoming skill activities as well as to remove distracting thoughts from their minds. It is usually employed at the beginning of a group and thereafter may be used periodically both preceding *and* following a particular skill exercise as the need arises to focus on feelings. It may be used any time to focus on underlying emotions.

How

Members may sit, stand, or lie down, whichever they prefer. They are instructed as follows:

"Close your eyes and relax your body as completely as possible. Breathe slowly and regularly. Now follow your thoughts for sixty seconds, not directing them in any channel or topic, just allowing them to go wherever they will. I want you to go along with them." (Sixty seconds of silence.) "Now, erase your thoughts, put all thoughts out of your mind and become aware of how you feel, not how you 'think' you feel, or would 'like' to feel, but your actual feelings and sensations as they are in the next minute. Dig deep. Experience. Be aware of the inside, don't think." (A period of several minutes.) "Slowly open your eyes."

A significant variation on the above is to instruct the members to become aware of each part of the body, starting with the toes. They then work up through the thighs, knees, buttocks, lips, eyes, hair, skin, etc. Each person is to try to "stretch" his awareness to include as great a body area as possible. The more parts they can become simultaneously aware of, the better. This variation is best accomplished with members stretched out on their backs, on a rug.

---

[1]Variations of this exercise are found in B. Gunther, *What to Do till the Messiah Comes*, New York: Macmillan, Collier Books, 1971. This description appears with the permission of author and publisher.

Results

Even if this first experience is successful, the leader should not press for any clear-cut response. It is best to allow those members to report on their feelings who spontaneously volunteer to do so. In the beginning, many members who have experienced some emotional response may be unable to or unwilling to put this into words. Their wishes should be respected, since talking may destroy what is essentially a nonverbal emphasis. Later in the life of the group, there should be less hesitation to share.

This structured experience may be used to focus on feelings when members have a sense of increased defensiveness due to underlying anxiety, anger, or even love at some time in the group. If the group members appear to be inadequately aware of their underlying feelings, having them stop and focus inwardly on these feelings may lead to very useful results. This activity provides data that result in having group members become more aware of their inner processes that influence overt behavior. In addition, it tends to result in legitimizing the discussion of personal feelings in the group.

5. SURRENDER AND SUPPORT
(B-5, B-31, B-33, M-9, M-10, M-11)

When

This intervention[1] may be given at any time during the group life, especially when an individual member is anxious, defensive, or in need of "stroking." It may also be used to strengthen emerging group norms of trust and intimacy. Intimacy involves joy in giving pleasure to someone and trust in accepting pleasure.

How

Shirley (following a monologue with illustrations of incidents in which people have let her down and how painful each situation was): "And I guess that's the reason I don't think that we'll get very close even in here. I would like to believe you, but it's hard for me to accept."

Group Leader: "Shirley, I want to suggest something that might be helpful now. Come stand here in the center. The rest of you join me in forming a circle around Shirley. It's important, Shirley, for you to keep your feet, knees, and lower legs firmly planted, but let the rest of you move wherever we move you. Close your eyes, relax the muscles in your body, and let your head fall back."

The group rotates Shirley until she seems comfortable and satisfied with the activity; then, as a variation, the other members may pick her up, holding her in a horizontal position, supporting her body so that all muscles can be relaxed, including the head. Members may place her at chest level or over their heads and gently sway her back and forth, lowering her until she is quietly and easily laid on the floor. Slowly the support and touching are withdrawn.

---

[1]This exercise has been utilized with many variations in encounter groups for many years. For other descriptions, see W. C. Schutz, *Joy: Expanding Human Awareness*, New York: Grove Press, 1967, pp. 181-186, and B. Gunther, *Sense Relaxation Below Your Mind*, New York: Macmillan, Collier Books, 1968, p. 160. This description appears with the permission of authors and publishers.

Schutz (1967) describes a variation of this exercise in which, after the person is placed on the floor, his muscles are stretched by three other members. The fourth member directs the activity. The recipient of this stretching is allowed to remain where he is as long as he chooses.

Results

When a person surrenders his whole body to others and finds that they will take care of him, he must examine his feelings toward them in a new way. It is a more direct expression than verbalization. Cooperating with others in the circle brings about a feeling of togetherness in the common task of giving pleasure to another. Verbal discussion of the feelings involved may be at the discretion of the subject. The leader should be prepared, at times, to simply allow the members to "sit with" the good feelings generated. This experience, if successful, usually dissipates sharpened anxiety or increased defensiveness. It will also promote the establishment of norms of group trust and intimacy.

6. THE GROUP SLAP
(B-5, M-9, M-11)

When

This structured experience[1] has its greatest value in those situations in which one or two members of the group have not achieved the tension release and level of relaxation of the other group members. Where it is desirable to relax those members and to demonstrate a feeling of group caring and loving, this experience has proved quite valuable. It seems to draw the member closer into the group and promote intimacy.

How (Variation 1)

Any even number from four to eight group members arrange themselves on both sides of the person to be slapped. The recipient of the slapping bends forward from the waist, torso parallel to the ground, legs well apart and braced, arms hanging loosely down. The slappers stand facing each other across his back. It is usually best to have not less than four people, two on each side. For maximum benefits, a third couple may stand at the recipient's rear and slap up and down the legs and buttocks. It is important that the entire back, buttocks, and legs be covered if possible. On a signal, everyone starts slapping in unison and in the same rhythm, covering all areas and trying to maintain the same slapping pressure among all slappers. This continues for about two minutes. This experience is ended by slowly and gradually easing up on the slapping until it fades away altogether. The slapping should be done with the open palm, both hands, and strong enough only to stimulate, not to cause pain. After the slapping is finished, the recipient remains bent over and feels the effect. Then he slowly straightens up.

---

[1]A variation of this exercise is found in B. Gunther, *Sense Relaxation Below Your Mind*, New York: Macmillan, Collier Books, 1968, pp. 182-183. The description of this exercise appears with the permission of author and publisher.

Results

This can be a very satisfying and emotionally involving experience if the recipient and the slappers are asked to be aware of their feelings toward each other and to express them nonverbally. With this added requirement, hugging, touching, and even a group "bear hug" are not uncommon. This is also a good experience in which to end a particular group meeting. The results appear to draw the group member into the group as well as to stimulate pleasurable feelings within that member toward the others.

A significant variation of the activity, in which the group divides into pairs for the slapping, is also useful.

How (Variation 2)

Each member of the group chooses a partner and stands behind him. The partner in front is instructed to relax and close his eyes. The partner standing in back focuses his attention on the shoulders of the person in front. (Thirty seconds are allowed for both to relax and settle.) The partner in back begins to slap along the entire edge of the person's shoulders from the neck to the arms. While slapping, the slappers are to allow their hands to take the shape of the area being slapped, wrists being loose and flexible: it is a vigorous but gentle slap that slightly stings but does not hurt. (Sixty seconds are allowed for slapping along the edge of the shoulders.) Then the leader gives these instructions:

"Now, move down his back, slapping the shoulder blades, evenly, both hands at once . . . now move down to the waist . . . back up to the shoulder blades . . . now, along the shoulders once more . . . this time, move down the entire length of the arms, all the way to the finger tips, and back up again . . . now, along the shoulder blades again and back down the arms . . . all the way down this time, along the waist and legs down to the feet and back up again."

These instructions may be repeated as often and for as long as seems necessary. The slappers should be instructed to end this exercise by slowly and gradually letting the slapping subside in intensity and frequency along the edge of the shoulders (a good stopping place). Finally the slapping is very light and gentle until it fades away altogether. The slapper puts his hands to his side and closes his eyes. Both partners are instructed to be aware of their feelings about both themselves *and* each other. After about sixty seconds they turn and nonverbally communicate their feelings toward each other.

7. GROUP OBSERVING GROUP
(B-7, M-7, M-13)

When

This structured experience may be used at any time when it is felt that the group as a whole would profit from breaking into smaller, more workable units, in order to study and deal with its own behavior. It is used to study group conflict and group processes, especially when cleavages or blockages seem to be present. It is usually less needed toward the end stages of group life since the members will have learned to deal skillfully with group processes by that time.[1]

How

The group is split, by any method appropriate to the conflict (dependent vs. counterdependent members, personals vs. counterpersonals, structure vs. counterstructure members, etc.), into two parts. One part arranges its chairs in a circle in the middle of the floor (in the "fishbowl"). The other group arranges its chairs in a larger circle around the smaller group. Both circles are facing inward toward the center of the circle. The inner group continues working on the group issues and concerns, as usual, while the outer group observes in order to gain additional insights as to the sources of blockage and to note the processes that seem to facilitate or impede group movement. After ten minutes, the groups switch positions such that the group members who were observing now become participants and vice-versa. At the end of the second ten-minute period, both groups come together as one large group to share their observations and discuss the relevance of this activity for the entire group.

---

[1]This exercise has been used for many years in NTL-IABS programs. This description appears with special permission from Learning Resources Corp./NTL.

Results

Some results of this structured experience include:

1. Group members are able to observe individual members' styles that facilitate or hinder group progress;

2. Group members are usually more prepared to recognize and pinpoint the areas of conflict and identify both surface and underlying issues; and

3. The experience provides the opportunity to observe common concerns that may outweigh differences, thereby helping members to come closer to managing conflicts better and making more effective decisions.

8. FANTASY IN ASSOCIATION (B-11, B-15, E-3)

When

This intervention may be used often throughout the entire group life but is intended primarily to deal with diffuse anxiety and with primary transferences/countertransferences toward the leader, or to illustrate the use of fantasy and symbolization to "sum up" some person. It encourages the creative use of fantasy symbolization and imagery as a means of "understanding" and "gaining insight into" another person or problem.[1]

How

A member or the group leader becomes the focus of this intervention in association by means of analogy. "If he were an animal, what kind would he be?" "What else does he remind you of?" "What smell is he?" "What sound?" "Describe him in terms of the elements; is he like the ocean, the mountains, the beach (etc.)?" "What kind of ocean is he like?" "What member of your family does he remind you of?" Another use for this exercise is in clarifying a problem, such as analyzing a person's commitment to the group, e.g., "Joe's commitment is like a plane with only one engine." In either of the above mentioned uses, analogy is utilized to cut through to the essence, by bypassing traditional factual and direct description. Caution should be given to give specific feedback about particular things the person can change. An analogy such as "He's like a blister on the ass of progress" does little to facilitate understanding, clarification, or change.

If the analogy is tied to a dynamic current in the group session, it is more effective. For example, if a group is finding it difficult verbally to deal with the group leader's authority, the leader might observe current behavior through the means of analogy and utilize the data for testing out feelings.

---

[1] See W. C. Schutz, "The Essence," in *Joy: Expanding Human Awareness*, New York: Grove Press, 1967, pp. 66–67, for another example of this approach. This description appears with the permission of author and publisher.

Group Leader: "I notice we are all sitting around with cans of Coke in our hands. If I were that can, what would you do with it?"

Some members may want to drop it or smash it, some may put it down, throw it away, drink from it, or put it on a pedestal. Detailed discussion about feelings following such an experience can serve to sharpen the focus of this intervention. The same technique, with minor variations, can be used at an instant's notice by the group leader's telling them first to pick up an object (pencil, pillow, piece of paper, etc.) and then saying, "I am that object. What do you now wish to do?" or "I am your left (right) hand. What do you feel? What is it communicating to you right now?"

Results

This experience is engaging and is very effective for stimulating analogies and associations. It demonstrates the principle of converting a feeling into a physical action as a vehicle for clarifying the feeling. It is often followed, most productively, by the intervention Peeling Emotional Layers. Everyone has the capacity to associate, sometimes to a remarkable degree. But the full use of this valuable ability requires a realization of its presence, the removal of emotional blocks, practice, and confidence that it works and can be a highly valuable aid to thinking, creativity, and increased awareness.

9. WHAT IS MY PLACE?
(B-13)

When

This intervention may be used to point up and underscore the power and authority concerns that are often present in the group. It may be used productively when issues of transferences/countertransferences seem to be operating just below the surface. In general, this experience may be used at any time in the life of the group when power and control issues are emerging. These frequently occur during the beginning to middle stages of the group.

How

The group leader states that he has an activity that may point up some of the difficulties the group is experiencing.

Group Leader: "I'd like all of you to line up in the middle of the room in order of importance. Look around at everyone else and try to decide where you think you belong in the line, based on whether you feel you're a more or less important person than whoever is next to you . . . O.K., can you do that now?"

Results

Usually very few, if any, group members will move to the center of the room. Some will be anxious. Some will welcome the opportunity to brag about where they should go. Some will be confused as to their proper place, and so on. After giving the group a few moments to digest how they feel in being requested to put their feelings into action, the leader should state:

"As far as I'm concerned, where you stand in line is meaningless. It's the emotions you felt while you were getting there and the way you made the judgments that count. Take you, Bill, you look at me and, 'bang,' you've got a reaction to me, just as you do to everybody. All our responses are determined partly by the way we come across, partly by our own emotional

reactions to a certain 'kind' of person, and partly by our feelings about ourselves—as in this experience. Let's talk about these responses for a moment."
This may precipitate a discussion involving leadership, authority, and feelings of self-worth.

10. THE NASA EXERCISE
(B-14)

When

This activity is best used whenever it is necessary to study the group decision-making process. It is essentially a task-oriented activity that requires all members to work together in reaching a consensus of opinion. It may be used to study emerging leadership, authority problems, decision making, or group performance, depending upon which facet is emphasized.

How

The leader reads the appropriate instructions from the NASA Instruction Sheet. He then hands out both the NASA Individual Tally Sheet and the NASA Group Summary Sheet so that each member may first make a personal choice and, finally, a group-consensus decision may be reached. The NASA Key gives the answers to this exercise. (See the Instruction Sheet, Individual Tally Sheet, Group Summary Sheet, and Key at the end of this description.)

Results

It is suggested that the group leader bring up the following questions as issues for discussion: "How quickly were you able to reach a personal decision as compared to a group decision? Did you ignore or utilize all the resources of the group in a decision? If there was disagreement over an answer, how was it resolved? How were dissenting members handled? Was there one leader, or more than one? How was leadership determined? Were you satisfied with the results?" The group leader may choose to focus upon one or more of the above questions for exploration in depth, or he may choose to direct the discussion into areas that were immediately present in recent critical incidents.

Special permission to reproduce the NASA Moon Survival Exercise is granted by the author, Jay Hall, Ph.D., and publisher of that material, Teleometrics Int'l. Copyright © 1963 by Jay Hall. All rights reserved and this material should not be reproduced without express permission of Teleometrics Int'l.

NASA INSTRUCTION SHEET

Instructions: This is an exercise in group decision making. Your group is to employ the method of *group consensus* in reaching its decision. This means that the prediction for each of the fifteen survival items *must* be agreed upon by each group member before it becomes a part of the group decision. Consensus is difficult to reach. Therefore, not every ranking will meet with everyone's *complete* approval. Try, as a group, to make each ranking one with which *all* group members can at least partially agree on. Here are some guides to use in reaching consensus:

1. Avoid *arguing* for your own individual judgments. Approach the task on the basis of logic.

2. Avoid changing your mind *only* in order to reach agreement and avoid conflict. Support only solutions with which you are able to agree at least somewhat.

3. Avoid "conflict-reducing" techniques such as majority vote, averaging, or trading in reaching decisions.

4. View differences of opinion as helpful rather than as hindering in decision making.

On the Group Summary Sheet place the individual rankings made earlier by each group member. Take as much time as you need in reaching your group decision.

Name _____

Group _____

NASA INDIVIDUAL TALLY SHEET

Instructions: You are in a space crew originally scheduled to rendezvous with a mother ship on the lighted surface of the moon. Due to mechanical difficulties, however, your ship was forced to land at a spot some two hundred miles from the rendezvous point. During re-entry and landing, much of the equipment aboard was damaged and, since survival depends on reaching the mother ship, the most critical items available must be chosen for the two-hundred-mile trip. Below are listed the fifteen items left intact and undamaged after landing. Your task is to rank order them in terms of their importance in allowing your crew to reach the rendezvous point. Place the number *1* by the most important item, the number *2* by the second most important, and so on through number *15*, the least important.

_____ Box of matches

_____ Food concentrate

_____ Fifty feet of nylon rope

_____ Parachute silk

_____ Portable heating unit

_____ Two .45 caliber pistols

_____ One case dehydrated Pet milk

_____ Two one-hundred-pound tanks of oxygen

_____ Stellar map (of the moon's constellation)

_____ Life raft

_____ Magnetic compass

_____ Five gallons of water

_____ Signal flares

_____ First-aid kit containing injection needles

_____ Solar-powered FM receiver-transmitter

NASA GROUP SUMMARY SHEET

Item	Individual Predictions of Each Group Member												Group Predictions
	1	2	3	4	5	6	7	8	9	10	11	12	
Box of matches													
Food concentrate													
Fifty feet of nylon rope													
Parachute silk													
Portable heating unit													
Two .45 caliber pistols													
One case dehydrated Pet milk													
Two one-hundred-pound tanks of oxygen													
Stellar map (of the moon's constellation)													
Life raft													
Magnetic compass													
Five gallons of water													
Signal flares													
First-aid kit containing injection needles													
Solar-powered FM receiver-transmitter													

Group ———————

NASA KEY

Little or no use on moon	15	Box of matches
Supply of daily food required	4	Food concentrate
Useful in tying injured together, helpful in climbing	6	Fifty feet of nylon rope
Shelter against sun's rays	8	Parachute silk
Useful only if party landed on dark side	13	Portable heating unit
Self-propulsion devices could be made from them	11	Two .45 caliber pistols
Food, mixed with water for drinking	12	One case dehydrated Pet milk
Fills respiration requirement	1	Two one-hundred-pound tanks of oxygen
One of principal means of finding directions	3	Stellar map (of the moon's constellation)
CO_2 bottles for self-propulsion across chasm, etc.	9	Life raft
Probably no magnetized poles, thus useless	14	Magnetic compass
Replenishes loss by sweating, etc.	2	Five gallons of water
Distress call when line of sight possible	10	Signal flares
Oral pills or injection medicine valuable	7	First-aid kit containing injection needles
Distress signal transmitter, possible communication with mother ship	5	Solar-powered FM receiver-transmitter

11. EYEBALLING
(B-16)

When

This intervention often illustrates the tension and anxiety we experience when looking at someone directly for even brief periods. It may be generally used to raise the anxiety levels of the members for more productive work. It has often been used with individuals who present a facade of coolness or universal love for everyone or to focus on feelings between two opposing members by emphasizing their feelings during this confrontation. This intervention should be used with discretion as it tends to raise the anxiety level and override any effects from immediately preceding exercises.[1]

How

Have each member of the group pair up with another member. They stand (or sit) in front of each other, about ten to twelve inches apart, staring into each other's eyes. They are not to smile, talk, or look away, and they are to concentrate on what's going on within them, not try to concentrate on some irrelevant topic to decrease the anxiety. The instructions are as follows:

Group Leader: "I would like each of you to look steadily and deeply into your partner's eyes. Try not to look away or talk during this experience. I want you to focus your thoughts on how this makes you feel, let the feelings grow inside you. Don't try to hold them back, just let them build and focus on them. Don't try to concentrate on anything except those feelings. O.K., start, and I'll let you know when to stop." (A sixty- to ninety-second pause.) "O.K., let's stop now and share our experiences."

---

[1]Variations of this exercise have been used in NTL-IABS programs and encounter groups for many years. This description appears with special permission from Learning Resources Corp./NTL.

Results

Usually, the group tension mounts dramatically. Often, anxiety-based laughter will begin, which serves momentarily to break the eye contact and release the tension. When the experience is finished, there may be explosive sighs and whistles over the anxiety generated. It is essential to share these feelings and to utilize this anxiety in some productive way, since it may be disturbing to some people. It may be used to point up the already existing sharpened anxiety in the group or to point up increased defensiveness.

12. RELEASING ANGER
(B-22)

When

The expression of hostile feelings is often inhibited by custom, fear of retaliation or embarrassment, or fear of one's own impulses. If this experience[1] can aid an individual in contacting his aggressive feelings and in expressing them productively, it can help to clarify and reduce these feelings. It may be used throughout the group life, whenever the need seems indicated, but especially where unexpressed underlying anger or intense affect appears to be present.

How

There are variations of this activity ranging from hitting a pillow to total body involvement such as that seen in body-therapy or regressive-therapy groups. Although the whole group may be performing the same activity, it is basically designed for individuals.

A member who is conflicted over expressing his anger and hostility is encouraged to act it out physically in a controlled situation. First, he may be asked to pound a pillow, to shadow box, or to put on soft padded gloves to use as clubs against the wall or floor. He is also told to use any sounds or words that help him get out the anger. If the hostility is directed toward another member or the leader, the object person is asked to hold the pillow. The purpose is to demonstrate to the member that his anger can be expressed without destruction or catastrophe.

Insights occurring during or following this activity are dealt with in the group after the anger has dissipated. Schutz (1967) adds another variant, that is, feeling the anger, getting ready to express it, and then holding onto the feeling without following through by striking. In some groups, to try to get in touch with suppressed anger, members work into or manufacture a rage by screaming, jumping on pillows, and hyperventilating. Linking this

---

[1]See W. C. Schutz "The Beating Exercise," in *Joy: Expanding Human Awareness*, New York: Grove Press, 1967, pp. 43-50, for a variation of this approach. This description appears with the permission of author and publisher.

experience to an actual incident or feeling expressed in the group will prove more effective than manufacturing the rage. Caution needs to be exercised in "opening up" a group member, and care needs to be taken in providing the appropriate closure to such a session.

Results

These exercises can have a very reassuring effect, which is often enhanced by later discussion. The person usually feels much freer to discuss his aggressive impulses after experiencing his own ability to control the impulses consciously. Subsequent talk may aid in draining off some of the long built-up tension. In this experience, as well as several others, the activity may seem false and artificial to begin with, but if it is continued, it usually becomes very real. It is important to continue despite the possible feeling of artificiality in order to experience the underlying affect.

13. BODY ENCOUNTER
   (B-22, B-25)

When

This category of experiences[1] may be used as needed to emphasize the assertive release of physical aggression, to relieve bodily tension directly, to promote and encourage actual encounters with other significant individuals. These experiences may be utilized during any stage of group life. They are especially valuable when words seem to be blocked. The following are some methods for bringing hostility and competition to the surface where they can be worked through. These are also applicable to other events reflecting sharpened affect and sharpened anxiety.

How

1. *Bumping.* An individual may be placed in the center of a ring of other group members. He then clasps his hands behind his back, hops on one foot, and, using body and shoulder contact, attempts to "bump" the others off balance. They attempt to return the action *only as they are approached individually* within the circle. An alternative is to have the individual choose the person he most needs to confront and have an individual-to-individual conflict. A minor variation upon this theme is to have the individual who feels "left out" to try and "bump" his way from the *outside* to the *inside* of a closed circle of fellow group members. At the other extreme is the individual who feels "boxed in" and must, accordingly, "bump" his way from *inside* a closed circle to the *outside*. Indian hand or foot wrestling may be used on an individual basis, as with bumping techniques.

2. *Arm wrestling* is another commonly used intervention in enounter groups for helping members explore the issue of power and control in a relationship and/or to foster involvement in the group. It is similar to Indian leg wrestling in that two group members lie opposite each other, locking right arms while resting on the right elbows. Each tries to force the other's arm to the floor without the use of other support and without moving the elbows.

---

[1]See W. C. Schutz, *Joy: Expanding Human Awareness*, New York: Grove Press, 1967, pp. 156-173, for a general approach to body encounters. This description appears with the permission of author and publisher.

3. *The press* is one of the most powerful experiences for exploring the power-dependency-competitive feelings between people. The press can help two people whose relationship contains unresolved negative elements. Two members face each other and place their hands on the other's shoulders. As they stand, they are given instructions to press the other participant to the floor. After one member is prone, the other is to help him back up. This, like the other exercises described here, is believed more effective if feelings, thoughts, and/or fantasies are dealt with in relation to the group following the activity.

4. *Pushing.* This is another variation of physical confrontation in which aggression or hostility is experienced rather than discussed. The hands are used both to apply pressure and to express resistance. The object is to gain ground and push the partner back. The degree and extent of the exercise are determined by the participants, the exercise being over when one member "gives in" or they both tire.

5. *The slap, the tap, the thump, the hip bump*—all are variations of this type of exercise. The object here, in contrast to the other exercises, is not to facilitate trust and affection, but to facilitate confrontation between two members or to confront a member with his lack of involvement or his "style" of involvement in the group, i.e., "hit and run," "overkill," etc. Caution should be taken to insure that there is no physical injury while experiencing emotional release.

Results

After they have finished, the participants and the observers usually want to talk about their reactions. It is valuable to have reactions to all four aspects of the situation: the feeling of subduing, of helping someone you have subdued, of being subdued, and of being helped. Often one of these four experiences (or variants) is much more salient than the other three. Frequently, there is much empathic reaction from the observers, and these reactions are valuable to explore. Ample opportunity should be allowed for a discussion of both individual and group feelings and an attempt at some partial resolution. This is an excellent "freeing-up" exercise.

14. EXPERIENCING CLOSENESS
(B-22, B-23, B-25, B-26, E-3)

When

This exercise is often used to "sharpen up" and define the underlying affect between two individuals and also cut through the facade of words by utilizing the whole body to expose genuine feelings and vulnerabilities of participants in a relationship.[1]

How

The participants are instructed to stand across the room from each other and slowly walk toward each other while retaining eye-to-eye contact. No other instructions are given except for them to relate spontaneously as they come together. Each is given permission to look and then act. The emphasis here is on spontaneity; therefore, the activity should continue until some semblance of this is evidenced or until the participants wish to stop.

A variation of this exercise is for the participants to sit opposite each other, encountering each other only with eye contact, and then decide how to respond spontaneously. The options include a physical response or a verbal response. This variation, of course, could be used as a dyad activity involving the whole group at the same time.

Results

After it is completed, the principals will ordinarily talk about their feelings, and the others will contribute their observations and identifications with the principals. Many variations appear and should be noted, such as which person wants to leave first, how uncomfortable each feels, if they embrace, whether they have a warm feeling or a way of avoiding looking at each other, who initiates the action, and so on. (See Structural Intervention 1, Empathic Communication.)

---

[1]See W. C. Schutz, *Joy: Expanding Human Awareness*, New York: Grove Press, 1967, pp. 140-143, for a comparable exercise, "The Encounter." This description appears with the permission of author and publisher.

15. SAYING GOOD-BYE
   (B-32)

When

This exercise[1] is generally more effective in the middle to late stages of a group. A climate of trust and a sharing of personal data and interpersonal skills by members and leader influence the results of the intervention.

A group member in some way shares the fact that the death of or rejection by a significant person in his life is painful and affects the way that he relates to other people in the present, even in the group. This "lost person" may be a parent, spouse, friend, lover, child, or other significant person and may or may not be alive. The dynamic involved is mourning, saying good-bye, and making peace with oneself while working through conflict about expressing feelings of anger, hostility, grief, and guilt.

How

This intervention utilizes two methods of psychodrama: *alter ego* and *role reversal.*

The member experiencing conflict is asked to pick someone to "be" the significant person. The meeting can take place in heaven, if the one being grieved for is dead; or in the past critical situation such as on the death-bed, back home. The vivid description of details can prove helpful in setting the mood. The role player attempts a realistic portrayal of the significant person. The member experiencing conflict adds to or takes over the role, switching chairs. Other members may act as alter egos. The closing scene may be a re-enactment of the event with as many members as possible participating—effecting a resolution. The emphasis is on the group member's expressing his real feelings and sensing the real feelings of the object of conflict. At that point an "adult" resolution is possible.

---

[1]See W. C. Schutz, *Joy: Expanding Human Awareness*, New York: Grove Press, 1967, pp. 81-90, "The Lost Person," for a variation of this exercise. This description appears with the permission of author and publisher. Also see J. L. Moreno, *Foundations of Psychotherapy*, 1959, for various uses of psychodrama techniques for facilitating grief work.

One variant of this activity is for the member experiencing conflict to play both parts, changing chairs, possibly with other members acting as alter egos later on in the exercise.

Results

This can be a powerful intervention and as such should be used with caution and by a skilled, experienced leader. For a person already "open and bleeding," this experience might prove too frightening for sufficient resolution. Time for an individual session with the leader may be indicated. However, this exercise has proved helpful to people dealing with mourning or unfinished business with a "significant other" or even an absent group member. Applicable to this exercise is the concept of "tension binding," that is, after bringing to the surface a certain conflict and working through it, the individual is helped to "let go" and reach an "adult" state for coping with the outside world. Implicit in this concept is the belief that one can "let it go," that is, bind tension until that person is able to work productively again. Thus, the exercise may need to be repeated one or more times for resolution, for the emotional transaction actually to be "finished."

16. AFFECTION BLANKET
(B-33, E-7)

When

The many variations[1] of exercises designed to help an individual to experience "massive affection" result in a powerful and emotional experience for the group as well as the participant. Therefore, this emotional experience is recommended for the later stages of group life.

As mentioned previously, the two sides of affection are joy in giving and trust in receiving. Many people experience themselves as unlovable, "not O.K.," or not worthy. The group can provide strong support for change in this area.

How

This exercise can be verbal and/or nonverbal. The object is to encapsulate the group member in affection and "unconditional positive regard." One method is for the group to give positive feedback to the member. He may be in the center of a circle, receiving eye contact and close physical contact along with the feedback, or he may sit with his back to the group and "eavesdrop" on the conversation. With either technique the recipient is simply to receive the information and sit with it.

The nonverbal exercise is accomplished by the member being the center of the group and receiving physical "stroking" of some nature, i.e., holding, rubbing, hugging, etc.

Results

Often after such an emotional experience the group members prefer to sit in silence with their feelings. Sometimes members seek out other members

---

[1]See W. C. Schutz, "Give and Take Affection," in *Joy: Expanding Human Awareness*, New York: Grove Press, 1967, pp. 176-180, and B. Gunther, "Resurrection Ceremony" and "The Laying On of Hands," in *What to Do till the Messiah Comes*, New York: Macmillan, Collier Books, 1971, for variations of this exercise. The description of this exercise appears with the permission of authors and publishers.

to whom they feel close. A word of caution concerns the person to whom touching is very threatening. Should a person express resistance to such an experience or be near tears before it begins, we believe some attention to the dynamics involved and group norms related to the right to say no is an effective means for both "testing the water" and instigating "tension binding" for the focal member of the exercise.

17. GROUP AND INDIVIDUAL JOURNEYS INTO FANTASY[1] (B-33, B-34)

Group Fantasy

When

This intervention may be utilized through the entire group life but seems most effective in the middle stages.

How

Group members may first crawl into a pile or come together holding hands as described by Gunther (1968) or simply lie down in a circle with heads or feet touching. Closing eyes and relaxing totally are the next step. The first member to relate his picture lays the foundation, and other members add to the fantasy. The object is for members to share in this journey together. The group leader may attempt to provide some direction for closure toward the end of the fantasy if this function is not assumed by another member.

Results

Since fantasy material is of a deep and powerful nature, some caution is suggested in selecting participants and in interpreting the content and symbols presented. Often members prefer to remain silent and then take a break or adjourn following this exercise.

---

[1]See W. C. Schutz, *Joy: Expanding Human Awareness*, New York: Grove Press, 1967, pp. 90-115, for a treatment of fantasy through exercises. This description appears with the permission of author and publisher.

Individual Fantasy

When

This intervention may involve the entire group but the focus is usually on an individual. When members seem defensive, inarticulate, or not in touch with their feelings, this exercise is a means of helping them focus on inner feelings and conflicts.

How

Again relaxation is a prerequisite. Some structural relaxation exercise may be used if needed. If one member is the focus, the leader instructs him to relax and then suggests an image to begin the fantasy: "Imagine you are in a dark room alone. What is happening? How do you feel?" Other images may also be used: "You are going on a journey alone. You are in a boat headed for an island. What is it like?"

Other leaders may prefer less direction: "Imagine you are in a beautiful place" or "You are free to be anywhere you want. Where are you? Describe it" or "You are free to build your own world. What is it like? What will you put in it?" It is important for the participant to share his feelings and thoughts. In a sense each is helping to guide the fantasy: the member with images and content and the leader with support, focus, and clarification of dynamics and feelings. When an entire group does an "inward focus" in fantasy, continuous feedback is unlikely. Therefore the leader may choose to start the fantasy by suggesting several other general steps and then a conclusion followed by mutual sharing of thoughts and feelings. For example:

Group Leader: "I want all of you to get as comfortable as possible. Just let your arms hang loose, your necks and shoulders relax and sort of draw into yourselves. Let's take a journey into fantasy. Let your mind go blank, and I'll start us off when everyone seems fairly comfortable. Imagine that you're floating in the Dead Sea. You can't sink. You're just floating, not having to do a thing. How does it feel? Get into it—sense how it feels to your skin." (Silence.) "The sun is shining warmly on your body. Can you feel it? Imagine how the shore looks, the sky . . ."

The extent of direction depends upon the abilities of group members to fantasize and the style of the group leader. Should this intervention uncover deep-seated fears or pain of a serious nature, the leader can lead a discussion of the dynamics involved, foster tension binding, and provide individual counseling following the session, if needed.

Results

Some caution should be exercised in both the leader's interpretation and in those individuals chosen to be participants in recognition of the potential material that may be uncovered. People may not want to talk immediately afterward. If the fantasy goes well, the participants have actually been living in the fantasy, and they sometimes take a while to return to the group reality. Silence followed by a break may allow time for the group members to assimilate their experiences and to shift moods to deal effectively with the dynamics later.

18. PEELING EMOTIONAL LAYERS
(B-32, B-34)

When

This intervention can be used as needed, but it is especially productive when it follows Fantasy in Association or Group and Individual Journeys into Fantasy.[1] This exercise is useful for those individuals who are rigid and find difficulty in getting in touch with their inner feelings. It is an attempt to explore underlying feelings directly, by focusing upon affect.

How

This may be conceptualized as peeling the skins off an onion, each layer being discussed as it is revealed. The group leader selects a participant and gives the following instructions:

"I want you to imagine that you, *yourself*, are composed of ten concentric circles, from the smallest at the core, to the largest, which is the outside part of you that everyone sees. First, tell us what you feel and see when you look at your outside circle. Describe the happy and sad parts of it, and then move on to the next inner circle. As soon as you are able, begin describing that to us. I will ask you questions from time to time and attempt to help you as you peel away the layers. Now close your eyes and relax. Picture the first, outer layer of the circle, the one everyone sees. Describe it to us, and tell us how it feels."

As the participant approaches the inner circles, the progress generally becomes slower and slower. Strong emotions of anger, sadness, weeping, and increased resistance may become evident long before the core circle is reached. It is not essential that the participant reach the innermost circle. It is up to the group leader to decide this, based on the perceived strength of the participant. It is essential, however, to deal completely with the emotions and thoughts engendered at each level of the circle *as they arise* and

---

[1]For a related activity see W. C. Schutz, *Joy: Expanding Human Awareness*, New York: Grove Press, 1967, pp. 134-136. This description appears with the permission of author and publisher.

not allow them to accumulate. If a person, for whatever reason, cannot go further than one or two levels, he may be allowed to rest before trying again, this time beginning at the last level he was able to reach.

Results

This is one of the most intimate and demanding of all the exercises. As such, it is subject to the cautions mentioned for all such skills: experience and good judgment are essential. The results, when thoroughly discussed afterwards, would appear to offer maximum value to the participant in terms of emotional cohesion with the group and a greater sense of emotional freedom.

19. EMOTIONAL SELF-SORTING
(B-27, B-29, B-30)

When

This structural intervention[1] is often quite useful when two or more group members are split over some intellectual or emotional issue. It may even be used when members are disagreeing over some surface issue but are not completely aware of the magnitude of the split within the group. The underlying emotionality in this activity is allowed to surface and demonstrate the polarization in the group.

How

It is strongly recommended that the group leader use this activity immediately following some conflict or heated interchange among two or more members. The instructions may go as follows:

Group Leader: "Without thinking too much about it, just moving according to how you feel right now, I'd like all of us to get up and move to any part of this room that seems appropriate. In other words, let your feelings direct you to do and go wherever you feel you most belong. Some of you might go to one corner, some to another, still others might remain seated or seek out another group. Don't think or deliberate too much, just go ahead and do it."

Results

Usually the group members split into groups that share the same attitudes and feelings. Other groups may consist of those who are uninvolved or neutral. Once everyone has found a group, each group's members describe their characteristics to the other groups. This usually leads to a distinct clarification of opposing positions. Finally, the leader should bring everyone back together to discuss the feelings involved, the merits of all viewpoints, and the possibility of utilizing divergent viewpoints to decide upon a common group direction.

---

[1]For a related activity, see W. C. Schutz, *Joy: Expanding Human Awareness*, New York: Grove Press, 1967, pp. 134-136. This description appears with the permission of author and publisher.

20. THE HAND PRESS
(B-31, M-10, M-11)

When

This exercise demands more trust in, confidence in, and exposure to the group and is usually best reserved for the middle to end stages of the group. It may follow The Group Slap or Surrender and Support.[1] Because of the confining nature of the exercise, those individuals with past difficulties at being restrained, held down, or confined may suffer some anxiety over this particular approach. Others will welcome it as a sign of group concern and love directed toward them. It should be utilized with caution.

How

The person who is designated as the recipient of the human blanket stretches out full-length on the floor on his stomach. He is to be as relaxed as possible. An *even* number of group members kneel beside the recipient, facing each other across his body (usually four to six people on each side is sufficient). In addition, one group member is stationed at the head and another at the feet, facing each other down the length of the body.

All group members shape their hands to conform to the contour of the section of body directly in front of them. They place their hands palms down about two inches above the person. At a given nonverbal sign from the group leader, everyone presses down firmly and gently upon the person's body. It is important that the person be touched by everyone at the same time. The person at the feet covers the soles of the feet, the person at the head covers the back of the head and neck. There is repeated firm but gentle pressure for about forty-five seconds with about thirty-second intervals in between. The object is to completely cover the body with a blanket of hands. The hands are not to be moved once placed on the body.

---

[1]For a variety of similar activities, see B. Gunther, *Sense Relaxation Below Your Mind*, New York: Macmillan, Collier Books, 1968, and *What to Do till the Messiah Comes*, New York: Macmillan, Collier Books, 1971. The description of this exercise appears with the permission of author and publisher.

After two presentations, it is best to have the person turn over on his back and to repeat the procedure above him from the front. If the subject is female, there should be no hesitation or exception: all parts of the body are to be covered, and this is to be understood and accepted if the person chooses to volunteer. Often this exercise is followed by the group's lifting the participant as described in Surrender and Support.[2]

Results

Usually there are a number of reactions, one of which may be anxiety (mentioned above). What is more likely, a sigh or smile comes across the face of the recipient, along with exclamations of intense pleasure and joy. It is generally a very emotionally binding experience between recipient and group members. Depending on the mood of the participants, they may or may not wish to discuss their experience.

---

[2]See B. Gunther, *Sense Relaxation Below Your Mind*, New York: Macmillan, Collier Books, 1968, p. 166, for a variation of this lifting procedure.

21. THE O-P-Q-R EXERCISE (M-1, M-2)

When

This structured activity is designed to be of specific help to an individual in the clarification and resolution of a stated problem.[1] It brings to bear on the problem three group members who question, record, or observe the participant's problem, thus making up a quartet of four members. The group leader may, at his option, decide to utilize more or less than this number, depending on the needs of the situation. It is a way of pinpointing specific problem areas, breaking down complex problems into smaller parts, and working on solutions. While this activity may be used at almost any point throughout the life of the group to work on an individual member's problems, it is most profitably employed during the middle to end stages. It may also be modified as an activity to help members get to know one another quite well.

How

The group is divided into one or more quartets, depending on the problems and members that need help. Each quartet is composed of the participant (who presents the problem), a questioner (who clarifies the issues and requests additional information), and an observer and a recorder who attempt to sum up and give specific concrete help. A significant variation of this activity is to use it in the group as a training exercise, allowing each member five or ten minutes in each role, before rotating and shifting roles to the next person in the quartet. In this variation, each member of the quartet has the opportunity to function as a participant, questioner, observer, and recorder, thereby sharpening his skills in each of these areas.

---

[1]This approach has been used in NTL-IABS programs for many years. This description appears with special permission from Learning Resources Corp./NTL.

Results

It is hoped that the use of this activity will (1) provide support and attention for members who have problems; (2) provide a more effective way of delineating and clarifying specific issues and concerns; (3) provide all members with training in a "helping relationship" role, thereby promoting a feeling of emotional cohesion, trust, and intimacy in the group.

22. BEHAVIOR PRESCRIPTION
(M-4, E-4, E-6, E-9, E-10, E-12)

When

This technique has found its greatest potential during the last stages of the group. It requires that the individual has had enough time and experience to be able effectively to utilize the prescriptions given to him. It has been found to have limited value in the beginning stages, due to individual resistance.

How

There are several methods of conducting this exercise. One method is to break the group into small units of threes, fours, or fives, depending on the size of the group. These small groups then move to individual rooms. Before the group is divided into appropriate subgroups and assigned to rooms or areas, instructions are given as follows:

Group Leader: "In order to facilitate some of the problems that we, as a group, have been struggling with, I want us to focus on the interpersonal issues that are involved. I would like us to explore ways in which we can aid each other in both individual and group productivity. It is, above all, a supportive and noncritical atmosphere that we wish to create. Here is how it works: in each group of three (or whatever the subgroup number), one person will leave the room for ten minutes. During that time the remaining members will first diagnose this person's typical style of interacting with others and secondly try to pinpoint *definite specific* helpful suggestions as to how this person might be helped to engage in atypical but productive behavior both for himself and the group. I must stress the terms *definite* and *specific*. Don't inform the person of some abstract generalization about himself, such as "You're too much of an introvert; try being an extrovert for a while," but give him definite and specific functions or behaviors to carry out that are generally atypical for him but productive. Thus, one person might be told to express his anger toward the group more directly and verbally instead of remaining quiet. After one person has been given his "behavior prescription," the next person leaves the room, and the process is continued until all have had their turn. We will all meet back here in 'X' minutes."

249

After the group has reassembled, there is usually little urging needed on the part of the leader to begin a discussion of the effects of this technique on various individuals. A significant variation is to have one person leave the room while all members focus their efforts on a behavior prescription.

Results

This is usually a very good technique to use, although it may require some closure by the leader for certain individuals whose composure has been shaken by a nonsupportive subgroup (although this tends to be infrequent). This technique is a significant variation of Structural Intervention 24, Last Impression. It enables an individual to "stretch" himself to fit another role and not to be afraid to try out a different behavioral style. It should be noted that these suggestions are given in a nonthreatening, supportive atmosphere that leaves the member free to respond as he feels appropriate.

23. HEAR MY "I"
(E-5, E-6, E-11)

When

This activity should be used only when group members have developed sufficient trust, emotional closeness, and decreased defensiveness so that they can participate openly and spontaneously.[1] It is therefore suggested that this structural intervention be utilized primarily during the late middle to end stages of the group. To introduce it earlier would probably lead to an anxiety-filled performance by all group members and offer minimal benefits. Introduction at the proper time, however, leads to an increase in intimacy and emotional cohesion among all group members.

How

The group leader instructs the group members to pick a partner and to sit facing him in a chair or on the floor, knee to knee. Depending upon the needs of the group at this particular time in the group's life, the leader may instruct group members to choose a partner "with whom you feel closest" or "with whom you feel a need to complete some unfinished business" or "whom you feel you know the least." Then the group leader gives the final instructions to all members.

"For the next three minutes I'd like one member to describe his partner by a series of sentences starting with 'I see.' Then, let your partner do the same to you for the same period. Next, start a series of sentences with 'I want . . .' for three minutes. Again, when you finish, let your partner do the same to you for the same period. Finally, start a series of sentences with 'I love . . .' for three minutes. After you switch roles for the last time and your partner has spent three minutes telling you what he loves, both of you sit quietly for about one minute. Finally, express, *nonverbally*, how you feel toward your partner. Then you may discuss the experience if you wish."

---

[1]The source of this exercise is "I See, I Want, I Love," B. Gunther, *What to Do till the Messiah Comes*, New York: Macmillan, Collier Books, 1971. The description of this exercise appears with the permission of author and publisher.

251

Results

This is an intensely emotional and potent exercise when used appropriately. There are usually two clearcut results:

1. Members become aware of intensely personal feedback that helps them understand how they come across to others; and

2. Members experience an increased feeling of intimacy, cohesion, and a generalized lowering of defenses. This atmosphere, in turn, better prepares the group for increased personal experimentation and growth.

24. LAST IMPRESSION
(E-5, E-9, E-10)

When

This experience is generally used at the end of the group experience to focus on *individual* resolved (and unresolved) feelings.[1] Ample time must be allowed for the resolution and closure of these feelings before the group is to disband, since this last procedure may turn out to be quite lengthy, depending upon the participants.

How

One way of exploring the impact that the group members have had on each other and the feelings involved is to start with each person, in turn, and have everyone in the group express his feelings (positive or negative) concerning the individual. The group leader expresses his feelings last. Then the next person is chosen, and the above procedure is repeated. The request is usually stated as follows:

Group Leader: "I feel we should devote some time to summing-up and closure. I would like to have us start with the person on my right and continue around the room, each person giving his thoughts, feelings, and conceptions of that person and expressing the need, if any, for dealing with unfinished business. After the circle has been completed, we will begin with the second person to my right and repeat the sequence, until everyone has had a chance. The person may or may not be in the center of the room, and others may approach him to look at him directly, or they may remain seated where they are. Often the group leader may have to interrupt the proceedings in order to deal with unresolved issues between the participant and another group member.

---

[1]Many group approaches have employed exercises of this kind, in particular the Gestalt approach. See also W. C. Schutz, *Joy: Expanding Human Awareness*, New York: Grove Press, 1967. The description of this exercise appears with the permission of author and publisher.

Results

This is an extremely powerful and potentially threatening exercise and very emotionally involving for all concerned. When it is over, there usually occurs what is termed "the love feast" or a great deal of expressed verbal and physical positive affect between each group member. (This may be contrasted with Structural Intervention 2, Early Perceptions.) Last Impression is often the final exercise in many encounter groups.

A Bibliography

Gunther, B. *Sense relaxation below your mind.* New York: Macmillan, Collier Books, 1968.

Gunther, B. *What to do till the Messiah comes.* New York: Macmillan, Collier Books, 1971.

Hall, J. *The NASA moon survival task.* Conroe, Tex.: Teleometrics International, 1963.

Moreno, J. L. *Foundations of psychotherapy* (J. L. Moreno, Psychodrama, Vol. 2.). New York: Beacon House, 1959.

Perls, F. S. *Gestalt therapy verbatim* (J. O. Stevens, Ed.). Moab, Utah: Real People Press, 1969.

Pfeiffer, J. W., & Jones, J. E. (Eds.). *A handbook of structured experiences for human relations training* (5 vols.). La Jolla, Ca.: University Associates, 1969-1975.

Schutz, W. C. *Joy: Expanding human awareness.* New York: Grove Press, 1967.

Appendix

OUTLINE OF CRITICAL-INCIDENT MODEL

I. Specify the Context Within Which the Critical Incident Occurred (Context of Incident).
   A. Specify the session number and the phase of the group: beginning, middle, or end.
   B. Specify the climate or mood of the group as it relates to the critical incident: dependent, counterdependent, unified, silent, hostile, depressed, etc.
   C. Give a brief description of the person(s) involved with each other and/or the group leader; specify both past and current behaviors.

II. Specify the Behavior and/or Conversation That Led Up To and Immediately Preceded the Choice Point (Event Preceding Choice Point).
   Group Member A: "I think the group leader should answer me."
   Group Member B: "I agree, and furthermore . . . "

III. Describe the Critical-Incident Choice-Point Situation as You Perceive It: Specify Both the "Surface Issue(s)" and the "Underlying Issue(s)" (Choice Point).
   A. Surface Issue(s):
   B. Underlying Issue(s):

   (What would you do at this point? Give rationale.)

IV. Specify the Level, Type, and Intensity of the Intervention Response (Suggested Intervention).
   A. Level of intervention (group, interpersonal, individual):
   B. Type of intervention (conceptual, experiential, structural):
   C. Intensity of intervention (low, medium, high):

V. Specify the Results of the Intervention on the Group (Intervention Outcome).
   A. The intended directional movement of the group:
   B. The actual group response to the intervention: silence, agreement, hostility, further developing critical incidents, etc.

257

MASTER INDEX

Theme Topics, Related Critical Incidents, and Structural Interventions

Theme Topic	Related Critical Incidents		Structural Interventions
1. Acquaintance			
The process of getting to know one another, to categorize . . . covert appraisal and testing . . . superficial acquaintances and information gathering.	B-1	p. 7	Empathic Communication (B-1, B-3), p. 205
	B-2*	p. 11	Early Perceptions (B-1, B-3), p. 207
	B-3*	p. 14	The Sharing Progression (B-1, B-5), p. 209
	B-4	p. 18	Introspection (B-4), p. 211
	B-5	p. 21	Surrender and Support (B-5), p. 213
			The Group Slap (B-5), p. 215
2. Goal Ambiguity and Diffuse Anxiety			
Lack of common goals and values generating anxiety . . . members seeking direction from leader and/or members and expressing frustration and anger . . . trivial, unrelated topics.	B-2*	p. 11	Group Observing Group (B-7), p. 217
	B-6	p. 24	Fantasy in Association (B-11), p. 219
	B-7	p. 27	
	B-8*	p. 30	
	B-9	p. 33	
	B-10*	p. 37	
	B-11*	p. 40	
	B-12*	p. 43	
3. Members' Search for Position/Definition: Primary Group Transferences/ Countertransferences:			
Competition among group members to please the leader and "protect" him . . .	B-8*	p. 30	Fantasy in Association (B-15), p. 219
	B-10*	p. 37	What Is My Place (B-13), p. 221
	B-11*	p. 40	
	B-12*	p. 43	

---

*More than one theme topic

seeking for the	B-13	p. 47	The NASA Exercise (B-14),
fatherhood of the leader	B-14	p. 50	p. 223
by desiring that he	B-15	p. 53	Eyeballing (B-16), p. 228
direct the group and	B-16*	p. 56	Group Observing Group
assume responsibility	B-17	p. 60	(M-13), p. 217
for what happens . . .	B-18	p. 63	
display of negativism	B-19	p. 66	
at the group's direction	B-20	p. 70	
and/or the leader himself	B-21	p. 74	
through resisting,	M-13	p. 158	
delaying, or disrupting			
behavior, often without			
acknowledgment of			
negative feelings.			

4. Sharpened Affects and Anxieties: Increased Defensiveness

Increase in both positive	B-3*	p. 14	Releasing Anger (B-22),
and negative affects, but	B-16*	p. 56	p. 230
primarily negative . . .	B-22	p. 77	Body Encounter (B-22,
cleavages beginning to	B-23	p. 81	B-25), p. 232
develop between	B-24	p. 84	Group and Individual
opposing factions—	B-25	p. 88	Journeys Into Fantasy
personals vs. counter-	B-26	p. 91	(B-33, B-34), p. 239
personals, structure vs.	B-27	p. 94	Experiencing Closeness
counterstructure, etc.	B-28	p. 97	(B-22, B-23, B-25,
. . . increasing anxiety	B-29	p. 100	B-26), p. 234
over disclosure and	B-30	p. 104	Affection Blanket (B-33),
increasing defensiveness	B-31	p. 108	p. 237
. . . much discussion of	B-32	p. 111	Saying Good-Bye (B-32),
goals and requirements	B-33	p. 114	p. 235
for inclusion in group	B-34	p. 117	Peeling Emotional Layers
. . . anxiety over	M-10	p. 148	(B-32, B-34), p. 242
expression of affect of			Emotional Self-Sorting
any type.			(B-27, B-29, B-30),
			p. 244
			Introspection (B-24, B-25,
			B-26, B-29), p. 211
			The Hand Press (B-31,
			M-10), p. 245
			Surrender and Support
			(B-31, B-33, M-10),
			p. 213

*More than one theme topic

5. Sharpened
Interactions:
Growth-Identifying
Activities and Reality
Strengthening

Members beginning to	M-1	p. 121	Empathic Communication
gain ability to	M-2*	p. 124	(M-2), p. 205
recognize and articulate	M-3*	p. 127	The O-P-Q-R Exercise
interactions with	M-4	p. 130	(M-1, M-2), p. 247
others . . . feedback	M-5	p. 133	Behavior Prescription
becoming more focused,	M-6*	p. 136	(M-4), p. 249

Members beginning to gain ability to recognize and articulate interactions with others . . . feedback becoming more focused, members becoming better participant/ observers who can look at group processes . . . increase in member participation . . . group beginning to respond helpfully to individual members, more reality testing and direct sharing of personal experiences.

6. Norm
Crystallization/
Enforcement –
Defensification

Development of reality-	M-2*	p. 124	Group Observing Group
oriented, workable	M-7	p. 139	(M-7), p. 217
norms dealing with	M-8	p. 142	Introspection (M-9), p. 211
control, intimacy,	M-9	p. 145	The Hand Press (M-11),
exposure, etc. . . .	M-11*	p. 151	p. 245

Development of reality-oriented, workable norms dealing with control, intimacy, exposure, etc. . . . deviant members assuming that certain necessary role functions, goals, and norms are used.

The Group Slap (M-9, M-11), p. 215
Surrender and Support (M-9, M-11), p. 213

---

*More than one theme topic

7. Distributive Leadership

Leadership becoming distributive in terms of functions and responsibilities assumed by members . . . personal problems explored in realistic manner . . . feelings of equality, support, intimacy among members.	M-11* p. 151 M-12 p. 154 M-14 p. 162 E-1 p. 165 E-2* p. 168 E-3* p. 171	Experiencing Closeness (E-3), p. 234 Fantasy in Association (E-3), p. 219

8. Decreased Defensiveness and Increased Experimentation

Relaxed defenses due to high support and trust among members able to experiment with new atypical behaviors . . . ability to deal with emotional issues directly, locus of evaluation moves inward to increase in self-awareness and insight.	M-3* p. 127 M-6* p. 136 M-11* p. 151 E-4* p. 174 E-5 p. 177 E-6 p. 180	Behavior Prescription (E-4, E-6), p. 249 Last Impression (E-5), p. 253 Hear My "I" (E-5, E-6), p. 251 Introspection (E-6), p. 211

9. Group Potency

Perception of the group as a potent, primary unit that is source of learning and growth . . . an intensification of affect into elation and excitement . . . members reward positive changes in others . . . ability to solve concrete problems.	E-2* p. 168 E-3* p. 171 E-4* p. 174 E-7 p. 183 E-8 p. 186	Affection Blanket (E-7), p. 237

---

*More than one theme topic

10. Termination

Expressions of over-
optimism and
sometimes depression
. . . attempts to deny or
prematurely withdraw
from group . . .
discussion of transfer
of group learnings to
real world.

E-9   p. 189
E-10   p. 192
E-11   p. 195
E-12   p. 198
E-13   p. 201

Behavior Prescription (E-9,
    E-10, E-12), p. 249
Hear My "I" (E-11), p. 251
Last Impression (E-9,
    E-10), p. 253